FamilyFun
Fast Family Dinners

100 Wholesome Kid-friendly Recipes
Your Family Will Love

EDITIONS

NEW YORK

FamilyFun Fast Family Dinners

FAMILYFUN
EDITORS
Deanna F. Cook
Grace Ganssle
Alexandra Kennedy

EDITORIAL ASSISTANTS
Jennifer Eastwood
Jean Graham
Heather Johnson

COPY EDITOR
Faye Wolfe

CONTRIBUTING EDITORS
Dawn Chipman
Mary Giles
Ann Hallock
Gregory Lauzon
Cindy A. Littlefield
Katherine Whittemore

PICTURE EDITOR
Mark Mantegna

PRODUCTION
Jennifer Mayer
Dana Stiepock

TECHNOLOGY COORDINATOR
Tom Lepper

IMPRESS INC.
CREATIVE DIRECTOR
Hans Teensma

DESIGN DIRECTOR
Carolyn Eckert

PROJECTS DIRECTOR
Lisa Newman

ART ASSOCIATES
Jen Darcy
Katie Winger

This book is dedicated to the readers of *FamilyFun* magazine.

All of the ideas in this book first appeared in *FamilyFun* magazine. *FamilyFun* is a division of the Walt Disney Publishing Group. To order a subscription, call 800-289-4849.

The staffs of *FamilyFun* and Impress, Inc., conceived and produced *FamilyFun Fast Family Dinners* at 244 Main Street, Northampton, Massachusetts 01060, in collaboration with Disney Editions, 114 Fifth Avenue, New York, New York 10011-5690.

Special thanks to the following *FamilyFun* magazine writers for their contributions: Rani Arbo, Lynn Bertrand, Cynthia Caldwell, Sharon Miller Cindrich, Joan Cirillo, Amy Cotler, Kathy Farrell-Kingsley, Linda Guica, Ken Haedrich, Amy Hamel, Ann Hodgman, Mollie Katzen, Mary King, Jeanne Lemlin, Elaine Magee, Shoshana Marchand, Catherine Newman, Jodi Picoult, Barbara Prest, Edwina Stevenson, Emily Todd, Michele Urvater, Stacey Webb, and Lynn Zimmerman.

We also would like to thank the following stylists: Bonnie Anderson/Team, Carol Cole, Holly Donaldson/Team, Shannon Dunn, Helen Jones, Janet Miller, Marie Piraino, Karen Quatsoe, Edwina Stevenson, and Lynn Zimmerman.

We extend our gratitude as well to *FamilyFun*'s many readers who shared with us their creative ideas. Thanks to Suzy Aydinel, Doris Creter, Julie Dunlap, Ruth Gill, Cathy Griffith, Kimberly Kroener, Amy Nappa, Charlotte J. Parcels, Candace Pease, Chandra Peters, Heather Sciford, Margaret Tindol, Lisa Weinstein, and Suzan L. Wiener.

This book would not have been possible without the talented *FamilyFun* magazine staff, who edited and art-directed the recipes for the magazine from 1993 to 2004. We also would like to thank our partners at Disney Editions, especially Wendy Lefkon and Jody Revenson.

ABOUT THE EDITOR:
Deanna F. Cook, Creative Development Director of *FamilyFun* magazine, is the editor of the *FamilyFun* book series from Disney Editions, as well as the author of *The Kids' Multicultural Cookbook* from Williamson. She cooks in her Florence, Massachusetts, home with her husband, Doug, and their girls, Ella and Maisie.

Contents

It's Dinnertime

WE KNOW WHAT it's like. The kids are raiding the fridge for snacks, your spouse just walked in the door, and the dog is looking at you with soulful despair. Dinner needs to get to the table — and fast — but how? *FamilyFun* to the rescue.

In the pages that follow, you'll find recipes for every kind of cook we know. These speedy dinner ideas work for the cook who starts planning dinner at 5:00 as well as the weekend chef who wants to get a jump start on the week ahead. All of our recipes can be prepared in under 30 minutes, but the cooking times vary from a 5-minute stir-fry to a 5-hour slow-cooker stew, so you can choose accordingly.

Oh, and did we mention that your kids might even like tonight's dinner, too? That's because our recipes are designed with picky eaters in mind, with fun touches and kid-friendly ingredients. Plus, we offer "Kids' Steps" with every recipe (to encourage budding chefs to lend a hand) and great mealtime tips from *FamilyFun* readers.

We don't recommend that you delete the pizza place from your speed dial. And we can't help with algebra homework or walk your dog. But we can help you whip up a healthy home-cooked dinner, with a little time to spare.

Stay ahead of weeknights. On a weekend afternoon, sit down with your kids and write out the menus for the week, before gathering ingredients at a supermarket or farm stand. Then, with as much help as you can get, do as much cooking as you can manage. Even one big pot of soup or stew will get you through Monday — and that means one less night of scrambling.

Make dinner together. With speed on your mind, it might seem counterintuitive to invite the kids to help — but do. Besides the fact that kids make great prep cooks — washing salad greens, for instance, while you cook the pasta — cooking together provides an opportunity to check in and catch up. And, come dinnertime, they'll more likely eat anything they helped make.

Eat dinner together. Quick and easy meal preparation means more time to spend with your family at the table. Turn off the TV, turn on your answering machine, and enjoy each other. Or try starting a weeknight tradition where everyone takes turns describing the best and worst thing about his or her day. Maybe dinner will even be the best thing about the day.

Make it special. It takes only moments to throw a pretty cloth over the table and light a candle or two, but these simple details can make dinner feel like a grand occasion — even if you're simply eating burgers or spaghetti. You might also try a weeknight surprise: serve breakfast for dinner or enjoy an indoor picnic in the family room to keep spirits high.

CHAPTER ONE

Soups & Salads

EVEN THE expression "soup and salad" evokes a quick, uncomplicated meal. And when it comes to cooking for kids, soups and salads are a classic case of the whole being greater than the sum of its parts. The ingredients — diced onions, slivered greens, cooked squash — will surely horrify your child, but offer him some Creamy Corn Chowder (page 16) or let him top his salad with crunchy croutons and cucumbers, and he'll eat everything up.

In addition to providing classic kid-pleasers like pasta and cheese, this cookbook gives you recipes for substantial salads featuring raw or lightly cooked vegetables. This means that not only will your children have crunch, color, and sweetness on their plates, but also that the ingredients move from fridge to table in a flash. The soups we offer are quick to assemble and make a satisfying opener to any meal or a wholesome, unfussy main course.

Take advantage of your grocery store's convenient offerings. These days, most supermarkets are teeming with time-savers: prewashed greens, sliced and chopped vegetables, packaged slaw mixes, good bottled dressings, canned broth, and more. By using them, you can have soup in the pot and salad on the table in minutes.

Invite your kids to help make soups and salads. The forgiving nature of soups and salads allows an extra touch of this and less of that to be added to the recipe, making it easy to include even very young kids in the cooking process. If your child is having a fine time peeling carrots, then more carrots may be peeled and thrown into the pot. If he picked a dozen cherry tomatoes from the garden, a big salad will use them all up. There are only a few irreparable mistakes your kids can make in the kitchen (like adding too much black pepper), but mostly, the recipes welcome creative additions.

Make it a meal. There's no law that says that dinner has to include a main course. Pair up a pot of nourishing soup with a colorful salad, then just add bread — try the Perfect Popovers (page 17), Easy Biscuits (page 45), or Buttermilk Cornbread (page 20), or an oven-warmed store-bought loaf — and you've got a satisfying meal on the table in no time.

Use leftovers creatively. Leftover salad need not go to waste. Those cut-up vegetables can be the basis of another nutritious meal. Use leftover veggies in tomorrow night's soup, garden-style pasta sauce, stir-fry, or fajita recipe.

Freeze an extra batch of soup. Soup is an ideal candidate for freezing, and making an extra-large batch takes only a little extra time. Double the recipe, then freeze half in plastic containers. Come a rushed, chilly evening, you'll thank yourself warmly!

At-home Salad Bar, page 8

FUN FOOD
Funny Face Salad

With a few garden vegetables, your junior chef can put a friendly smile on his salad. Hand him a plate of fresh greens; then he can add tomato and cucumber eyes, grated carrot hair, hard-boiled egg ears, and rosy red pepper cheeks (cut with a tiny cookie cutter). Serve dressing on the side for dipping.

FOR A QUICK AND healthy appetizer or complete dinner, invite your kids to help set up a restaurant-style salad bar. The best part about a salad bar is that anything goes: fresh greens, raw veggies and toppings, leftovers, and sliced bread. For variety (and to make sure your kids eat a well-balanced meal), arrange the food in the following groups and encourage everyone to choose at least a couple of ingredients from each. Put out store-bought or homemade salad dressings (see our easy-to-make dressings at right).

INGREDIENTS:
GREENS
    Romaine or iceberg lettuce, mesclun, spinach, or Swiss chard
VEGETABLE TOPPINGS
    Bell peppers, mushrooms, shredded red cabbage, cherry tomatoes, or carrot sticks

PROTEIN ADD-INS
    Grated cheese, smoked turkey or ham cubes, salami strips, chickpeas, or hard-boiled eggs

SPOON-ONS
    Chopped peanuts, pine nuts, croutons, pitted olives, raisins, or sunflower, pumpkin, or sesame seeds

DIRECTIONS:
Chop vegetables and tear lettuce up to a day or two ahead of time.

Refrigerate them separately in plastic bags poked with holes — which lets oxygen in and prevents spoilage.

When you're ready to eat, transfer the fixings to serving bowls set on the table. Serve with one of the following salad dressings.

PARMESAN VINAIGRETTE
This quick mix is delicious and creamy. Using a blender, combine 1 cup corn or olive oil, 1 cup freshly grated Parmesan or sharp Cheddar cheese, 2 tablespoons white wine vinegar, ½ cup low-fat plain yogurt, 1 tablespoon Dijon mustard, and salt and pepper to taste, until creamy and smooth. Pour into a bowl, cover, and store in the refrigerator. Makes about 2 cups.

GARDEN GREEN SALAD DRESSING
The secret to this dressing is a good, fruity extra-virgin olive oil. Measure 2 ounces balsamic vinegar and 4 ounces extra-virgin olive oil into a small sealable jar. Add l teaspoon salt and l garlic clove, minced. Close and shake. The leftover dressing can be stored in the refrigerator. Makes ¾ cup.

RANCH DRESSING
For this creamy, kid-friendly dressing, whisk 6 tablespoons of sour cream, 6 tablespoons of milk, and 1 teaspoon white vinegar in a small mixing bowl. Add ½ teaspoon garlic powder, 1 tablespoon parsley flakes, 1 teaspoon dill, a pinch of salt, and a dash of pepper. Chill for at least 30 minutes. Makes ¾ cup.

KIDS' STEPS: Kids can wash and tear the fresh greens, chop softer vegetables with a plastic knife, and place the salad bar items in bowls on the table.

Prep time: 15 to 30 minutes

Crunchy Carrot Salad

FOR A COLORFUL salad that will enliven any dinner plate, you can't beat this light and tasty side dish. It will retain its delightful crunch for a day or two, so you can enjoy it for two nights — just sprinkle on a few drops of lemon juice and olive oil before serving to enhance the flavors. For the best results, use California carrots, which tend to be sweeter than Canadian carrots. As a time saver, purchase grated carrots at your supermarket.

INGREDIENTS:

1   pound carrots, peeled
¾   cup dry-roasted unsalted peanuts
3   tablespoons minced fresh parsley
2   tablespoons finely chopped fresh mint
¼   cup olive oil
2   tablespoons fresh lemon juice
1½ teaspoons sugar
¼   teaspoon salt

DIRECTIONS:
Grate the carrots on the coarse side of a box grater (a food processor will make the carrots too soft for this salad).

In a large bowl, gently toss together the carrots, peanuts, parsley, and mint. In a small bowl, thoroughly stir together the olive oil, lemon juice, sugar, and salt, then pour the dressing onto the salad and toss again until the carrots are evenly coated.

Let the salad stand for 20 minutes before serving, or refrigerate it and eat within 2 days. Serves 6.

KIDS' STEPS: Older kids can wash, peel, and grate the carrots and measure and mix the dressing.

Prep time: 20 minutes

Spinach Salad with Pine Nuts

LIGHT, CRISPY, AND healthful, this spinach salad is a kid and parent pleaser. "It's the only salad I can eat without dressing," says *FamilyFun* reader Candace Pease, whose mom invented it when Candace was growing up in Santa Ana, California. The roasted pine nuts complement the turkey bacon (regular bacon works fine, too), and the mandarin oranges add a little extra zing. Serve this salad as a side dish to grilled turkey or chicken.

INGREDIENTS:

- ¼ cup pine nuts
- 8 slices turkey bacon, cooked and crumbled
- 8 ounces baby spinach, washed and dried
- 1 15-ounce can mandarin oranges, drained
  Dressing, such as Garden Green Salad Dressing, page 8 (optional)

DIRECTIONS:

Heat the oven to 350°. Roast the pine nuts on a baking sheet for 5 to 8 minutes, until they turn golden brown, then allow them to cool.

Toss together all of the ingredients in a large salad bowl just before serving — do it any sooner and the bacon and pine nuts will lose their crispness. (If you like, you can store the prepared ingredients separately in plastic bags.) Serves 8.

KIDS' STEPS: Kids can wash and tear the spinach, add the mandarin oranges, and toss the salad.

QUICK HIT
A Berry Good Salad

For a kid-friendly spinach salad, whisk together ½ cup of vegetable oil, ¼ cup of white vinegar, ¼ cup of sugar, 1 tablespoon of poppy seeds, ¼ teaspoon of paprika, and ¼ teaspoon of salt in a medium bowl. Add the dressing to 6 ounces of fresh baby spinach leaves mixed with 4 cups of sliced strawberries, tossing until well combined. Serves 6.

Prep time: 20 minutes   Cooking time: 8 minutes

Corny Bean Salad

THIS IS NO ordinary bean salad. It brings into play all the sunny flavors and colors of summer: the yellow cheer of fresh corn, the sweet crunch of red bell peppers, and the bright green hit of cilantro. Kids seem to love the mellow richness of black beans, but use whichever beans your family likes best. For a complete meal, serve this with Chicken Quesadillas (see page 41).

INGREDIENTS:
SALAD:

- 3 15-ounce cans beans (choose a variety from garbanzo, red kidney, white kidney, black, and pinto)
- 1 cup corn, fresh or frozen, cooked and cooled
- ½ red pepper, chopped
- 2 slices red onion, chopped
- ¼ cup chopped fresh cilantro

VINAIGRETTE:

- 6 tablespoons olive oil
- 2 tablespoons balsamic vinegar
- 1 teaspoon Dijon mustard
  Salt and pepper to taste

DIRECTIONS:

Drain and rinse the canned beans, then place them in a large bowl. Add the corn, red pepper, red onion, and cilantro and stir.

Next, prepare the vinaigrette. Measure the olive oil, vinegar, and mustard into a jar. Screw on the lid tightly and shake the dressing well. Add salt and pepper to taste. Pour the vinaigrette over the beans a little at a time and mix to coat. Add enough vinaigrette to suit your taste. Refrigerate the salad until you are ready to serve. Serves 8 to 10.

KIDS' STEPS: Kids can rinse the beans, stir the salad, and mix up the vinaigrette dressing.

MY GREAT IDEA
Mosaic Munchies

"When dinnertime runs late at our house, my kids, ages two and nine, tend to get hungry and a little impatient. Finally, I found a way to appease them while they wait — an appetizer and craft activity in one. I give them each two crackers spread with cream cheese and a bowl of raisins, peanuts, or vegetables, and they create edible mosaics while I prepare dinner. After giving a quick showing, they gobble up their masterpieces."

— *Cathy Griffith*
Madeira Park, British Columbia

Prep time: 15 minutes

Something-for-Everyone Tortellini Salad

WITH THREE LITTLE BOYS to feed, *FamilyFun* food writer Mary King is always challenged to find a recipe that pleases everyone. The kids' tastes range from adventurous (her oldest) to "nothing but pasta with cheese will pass these lips" (her baby), to somewhere in between (her middle guy). One food they all love, however, is tortellini, and this highly adaptable dinner salad lets Mary keep everyone happy. She sets aside a portion just tossed with butter, and the rest gets dressed up into a salad that can be adjusted to suit individual tastes.

INGREDIENTS:

- 1 pound cheese tortellini
- 18 cherry tomatoes, cut in half
- 1 cucumber, thinly sliced
- ½ pound fresh mozzarella, cubed
- 2 tablespoons chopped fresh basil
- 1 avocado, sliced
- ¼ cup olive oil
  Juice of 1 lime
- 3 tablespoons balsamic vinegar
  Salt and pepper

DIRECTIONS:
In a large pot, bring 3 quarts of water to a boil. Add the tortellini and gently boil for 7 to 9 minutes or until tender, then drain and rinse under cold water. Transfer the cooked tortellini to a serving bowl and add the tomatoes, cucumber, cheese, basil, and avocado.

Combine the olive oil, lime juice, and balsamic vinegar; add salt and pepper to taste. Drizzle over the salad and toss to combine. Serves 6.

KIDS' STEPS: Kids can cut the cherry tomatoes in half with a plastic knife and cut the basil with (clean) scissors.

Prep time: 30 minutes   Cooking time: 9 minutes

New Potato Salad

THIS OLD FAVORITE gets its creamy texture not from mayonnaise, but from its mustard vinaigrette dressing combined with bits of hard-boiled egg. For a quick cookout dinner, serve this potato salad with the Better Burgers, page 27.

INGREDIENTS:
- 4 pounds new potatoes, unpeeled
- 6 tablespoons cider vinegar
- 4 tablespoons chicken broth
- ½ cup vegetable oil
- 3 tablespoons Dijon mustard
- ¼ cup minced onion
- 4 hard-boiled eggs, finely chopped
- 4 stalks celery, finely chopped
- 2 teaspoons salt
- Black pepper to taste

DIRECTIONS:
Boil the potatoes in a large pot of water for about 30 minutes, or until tender. Do not overcook. Drain and set aside for about 20 minutes. In a large bowl, combine the cider vinegar, broth, vegetable oil, mustard, onion, eggs, celery, salt, and pepper.

Slice the warm potatoes and toss with the dressing mixture until well coated. Cover and let marinate for 1 hour. Refrigerate for up to 2 days. Serves 8.

KIDS' STEPS: Kids can wash the potatoes, mix the dressing, and peel and slice the hard-boiled eggs.

**Prep time: 15 minutes   Marinating time: 1 hour
Cooking time: 30 minutes**

Creamy Corn Chowder

RICH, CREAMY CHOWDER IS a favorite comfort food dinner — reassuring, full-bodied, and delicious. And it's easier to make than a lot of cream soups because you don't have to puree anything. Our crusty popovers (page 17) taste great dipped in this soup.

INGREDIENTS:
- 2 tablespoons butter
- 1 large onion, finely chopped
- 1 rib celery, finely chopped
- 5½ cups chicken stock
- 1½ cups frozen corn kernels
- 1 large all-purpose potato, peeled and diced
- ½ to ¾ teaspoon salt, to taste
- 1 cup heavy cream
- 3 tablespoons all-purpose flour
  Black pepper, to taste
  Fresh dill or parsley for garnish, chopped

DIRECTIONS:
Melt the butter in a large saucepan or medium soup pot. Stir in the onion and celery. Partially cover the pan and cook the vegetables over moderate heat for 9 to 10 minutes, stirring occasionally.

Add the chicken stock, corn, potato, and salt and bring the mixture to a low boil. Lower the heat, cover the pot, and simmer for about 7 minutes, until the potatoes are just tender.

In a small bowl, whisk together the cream and flour. Then stir the mixture into the soup with the pepper. Bring the soup back to a low boil, then reduce the heat and simmer for about 8 minutes, stirring occasionally. Serve hot, garnished with herbs. Makes 5 to 6 servings.

KIDS' STEPS: Older kids can help peel and cut the potato and measure the soup ingredients.

Prep time: 30 minutes   Cooking time: 30 minutes

Tortellini and Bean Soup

THE COMBINATION OF pasta and beans makes a hearty meal, just right for a chilly fall evening. Serve with a loaf of warm, crusty French bread or Perfect Popovers, at right, and grated Parmesan cheese.

INGREDIENTS:

3   tablespoons olive oil
1   medium onion, chopped
1   garlic clove, crushed
1   cup canned chopped tomatoes, drained
8   cups canned low-salt chicken broth
1   teaspoon each dried oregano and basil
3   15-ounce cans black beans, rinsed and drained
2   tablespoons rice vinegar
    Black pepper, to taste
12 ounces fresh or frozen cheese tortellini

DIRECTIONS:
In a large soup pot, heat the olive oil over medium heat. Add the onion and sauté for 3 minutes. Add the garlic and drained tomatoes and cook for 3 minutes. Add the chicken broth, oregano, basil, drained black beans, vinegar, and black pepper.

Reduce the heat to low and simmer for 5 minutes. Finally, add the tortellini to the soup and cook for 8 minutes or until tender. Serves 8.

KIDS' STEPS: Older kids can help open the cans and rinse and drain the beans.

BREADS WE LOVE
Perfect Popovers

If your kids have never seen popovers bake, they'll be amazed at how the simple batter dramatically puffs up into such a crisp and delicious treat.

In a medium bowl, whisk 2 large eggs until frothy, then whisk in 1 cup milk and 1 tablespoon vegetable oil (great jobs for a kid). Combine 1 cup all-purpose flour and ¼ teaspoon salt and sift into the liquid, whisking to make a smooth batter. Let the batter rest for 10 minutes. Meanwhile, heat the oven to 425° and lightly butter 6 popover cups or 8 muffin cups.

Whisk the batter again and pour it into the buttered cups (about two-thirds full), dividing it evenly. Bake for 30 minutes or until tall and dark golden. *Do not* open the oven before 30 minutes have passed — you can check on them after that. Once they're done, immediately remove them from the oven and use a thin skewer to poke a hole in each one to let out steam. Serve at once. Makes 6 to 8.

Prep time: 15 minutes   Cooking time: 20 minutes

Soup Sous-chefs

Making soup is a cooking lesson that can grow as your kids do. Because most soup recipes require a variety of basic skills from chopping to sautéing, it's a good chance for kids to learn under your watchful eyes. Here are a few tips to get them safely under way.

- Kids ages three and up can start by learning to cut softer vegetables with a plastic knife. Kids over eight can begin learning to use a paring knife.

- If kids are stirring the soup or sautéing, turn the pot handle toward the back of the stove so there's no danger of their tipping it.

- Let kids try snipping fresh herbs into the soup, using kitchen scissors. Show them how to adjust the seasoning after it has simmered. Take a spoonful from the pot, blow on it until it's cool, then taste the soup. Does it need more salt? Pepper?

- For an easy beginner recipe, try preparing ramen noodle soup mix according to the package directions. Then, have kids add in their favorite vegetables, such as frozen peas, sliced mushrooms, and a diced tomato.

Butternut and Ham Bisque

THIS ONE-POT MEAL offers one of the garden's most distinctive flavors: sweet winter squash. To save time, purchase peeled and cubed squash at your farmer's market or grocery store.

INGREDIENTS:

- 2 tablespoons unsalted butter
- 1 large sweet onion, chopped
- ½ teaspoon dried rosemary leaves, chopped
- 2 garlic cloves, crushed
- 5 cups peeled and diced butternut squash
- 1 cup peeled and diced all-purpose potatoes
- 5 cups chicken stock
- 1 teaspoon salt
  Black pepper, to taste
- ½ cup light or heavy cream
- 1½ cups diced cooked ham

DIRECTIONS:

Melt the butter in a medium-size soup pot or a large saucepan. Stir in the onion and rosemary. Partially cover the pan and cook the onion over moderate heat for 10 minutes, stirring occasionally. Stir in the garlic and cook another minute.

Add the squash, potatoes, chicken stock, and salt and bring to a boil. Reduce the heat and cover the pot. Cook the soup at a low boil for 20 minutes or until the vegetables are very soft. Remove the pan from the heat.

Using a large slotted spoon, transfer the soup solids and a ladleful of broth to a food processor (do this in batches if your processor is small). Puree the vegetables, then stir them back into the broth. Stir in the pepper, the cream, and the ham, heating for several minutes before serving. Makes 6 servings.

KIDS' STEPS: Kids can measure ingredients, peel and chop the squash and potatoes, and crush the garlic with a garlic press.

Prep time: 15 minutes   Cooking time: 40 minutes

Buttermilk Corn Bread

For a subtly sweet complement to the chili at right, serve this skillet-baked corn bread.

Heat the oven to 400°. Put 3 tablespoons butter in a 10-inch cast-iron skillet (or a 10-inch deep-dish pie pan) and place it in the oven while you prepare the batter.

Sift 1 cup all-purpose flour, 1 cup fine yellow cornmeal, 2 tablespoons sugar, 1 teaspoon baking soda, 1 teaspoon baking powder, and 1/2 teaspoon salt into a large bowl. In a separate bowl, blend 2 large eggs, lightly beaten, and 2 cups buttermilk.

When the butter has melted, remove the skillet from the oven. Swirl the pan to spread the butter, then pour most of the butter into the liquid ingredients. Make a well in the dry ingredients and add the liquid. Stir the batter until evenly mixed, then pour it into the hot skillet.

Bake the bread for 25 to 30 minutes or until the top is golden and crusty, then cool it in the pan on a wire rack for 10 minutes before slicing. Makes 10 servings.

Beef and Black Bean Chili

HERE'S A FULL-FLAVORED chili with just a touch of heat. If your kids don't like theirs too spicy, use only about three-quarters of the Southwest Seasoning Mix (see below) and save the rest to season other Tex-Mex dishes.

INGREDIENTS:

- 1/2 pound ground beef
  Vegetable oil
- 1 large onion, chopped
- 1 medium green bell pepper, chopped
- 1 garlic clove, minced
- 3 tablespoons Southwest Seasoning Mix (see below)
- 1 1/2 cups V8 or tomato juice
- 1 1/2 to 2 cups beef or chicken stock
- 1 cup canned crushed tomatoes in puree
- 3 to 4 cups cooked black or red beans
- 3/4 teaspoon salt
  Black pepper, to taste
  Grated Cheddar cheese
  Sour cream
  Chopped parsley, for garnish

DIRECTIONS:

In a medium-size soup pot, brown the ground beef over medium heat for several minutes. Using a slotted spoon, transfer the meat to a small bowl and set it aside.

If there's very little fat left in the pan, add 1 to 2 tablespoons of vegetable oil; if there's too much, spoon some out. Add the onion and green pepper and sauté over moderate heat for 8 to 9 minutes, until the onion is translucent. Add the garlic and Southwest Seasoning Mix, stirring constantly for 30 seconds.

Stir in the tomato juice, stock, canned tomatoes, beans, salt, and pepper, and the reserved meat, using enough stock to achieve a consistency that is neither too thin nor too thick. Bring the mixture to a boil. Cover the pot, then reduce the heat and simmer gently for 10 to 15 minutes, stirring often. Thin the chili with a little more stock if necessary. Serve hot with the toppings and garnish. Serves 6.

SOUTHWEST SEASONING MIX

In a bowl, mix together 1 tablespoon cumin, 1 tablespoon mild chili powder, 1 1/2 teaspoons coriander, 1 teaspoon dried oregano, 1 teaspoon unsweetened cocoa powder, and 1 teaspoon sugar.

KIDS' STEPS: Kids can measure and mix up the Southwest Seasoning Mix, rinse the beans, and set out the toppings in bowls.

Prep time: 20 minutes Cooking time: 30 minutes

CHAPTER TWO

Main Courses

EVERY FAMILY COOK needs a collection of kid-friendly meals that can be pulled together in record speed. So in this chapter, we proudly present our own secret stash of quick hits. These main dishes are easy to prepare and offer both picky-eater appeal and a healthy dose of nutrition.

Thankfully, some of the foods kids like the most — pizza, spaghetti, and burgers — are also some of the quickest and simplest to prepare. Here, you'll find healthy, homemade fast foods, such as The Better Burgers (page 27) and crispy Chicken Tenders (page 42) to add to your family's repertoire. Plus, many of our recipes, such as Steak Stir-fry (page 33), Chicken Fajitas (page 41), or Pasta with Pesto (page 58) offer a quick trip to the kid-pleasing cuisines of other cultures — proving, of course, that Americans aren't the only people trying to get dinner on the table in a hurry!

Adapt the recipes to suit your family's preferences. By all means, alter these recipes to accommodate your family's tastes. Picky eaters at home? Nix the spices or keep some veggies out of the stir-fry and serve them raw. Cutting back on red meat? Substitute ground turkey for beef. Vegetarians in your household? Omit the meat in a recipe and use tofu or tempeh instead.

Double the recipe. Cook up an extra batch of chicken — or beef stew or spinach lasagna — tonight, and, come tomorrow night, you've got an easy dinner ready. All you have to do is heat up the leftovers. If your family can't stomach the same meal two nights in a row, pop the leftovers in the freezer and have them next week. Or transform them into a new dish (see Chicken Quesadillas on page 41 which uses leftover Chicken Fajitas).

Change with the season. In the summertime, pair a classic grilled steak (page 32) or our delicious Easy Dry Rub for chicken (page 47) with one of our fresh garden salads (page 8), and you've got dinner on the table fast. When the days turn cold, turn on the slow cooker instead. A few minutes spent prepping ingredients in the morning means you come home to the warming Best Ever Beef Stew (page 36), mouthwatering Pork on a Bun (page 30), or unexpected Mu Shu Chicken Wraps (page 40).

Entertain easily. Whether it's a houseful of weekend guests, friends dropping by unexpectedly, or a school potluck, you're bound to be faced with the occasional crowd to feed. Many of the recipes in this chapter are inexpensive, easy to multiply, and fine to make ahead of time. Or like the fabulous Shrimp on a Stick (page 53), they offer near-instant elegance. That means less last-minute scrambling and more time to enjoy your company.

Think inside the lunch box. Cook up extra steak or chicken breast, and, come morning, you've got an easy lunch to pack for the office or school. Ditto pizza, which kids (and many adults!) love to eat cold, and meat loaf and roast chicken, which make terrific sandwiches. Consider this in your choice of sides as well: pasta- and bean-based salads both travel beautifully in lidded containers.

Shrimp on a Stick, page 53

Soft Beef Tortillas

QUICK HIT
Creamy Guacamole

The soft texture and subtle flavor of guacamole make this favorite Mexican dip a hit even with young children. Serve it with tortilla chips or the Soft Beef Tortillas at right.

Peel and chop 3 ripe avocados and place the pieces in a small mixing bowl. (Reserve one of the avocado pits.) Using a fork, mash the avocados until you have a creamy mixture. Stir in the juice of 1 lime. Add 2 tablespoons of minced onion, 1 crushed garlic clove, $^1/_2$ teaspoon pepper, and $^1/_2$ teaspoon salt and mix well.

For a zestier dip, stir in $^1/_2$ cup store-bought salsa. Guacamole is best served within an hour or so of making it, since it turns brown quickly. Put the reserved avocado pit in the guacamole to slow this process. Makes about 2 cups.

IF MEXICAN FOOD is the rage in your household, mix up this not-too-spicy homemade taco filling. We've given the classic dish a healthy twist by wrapping the filling in a soft tortilla instead of a fried shell. At the table, the kids get to pick their own toppings.

INGREDIENTS:

- 2 tablespoons vegetable oil
- ½ small red onion, minced
- 1½ pounds ground beef
- 2 garlic cloves, crushed
- 1 tablespoon chili powder
- 1 teaspoon cumin
- 1 teaspoon coriander
- 1 teaspoon salt
- 1½ cups tomato sauce
- 10 flour tortillas

TOPPINGS:

- ½ small head iceberg lettuce, shredded
- 1 cup Monterey Jack cheese, shredded
- 1 small yellow or red bell pepper, sliced
- 1 cup canned black beans, rinsed
  Salsa and guacamole (see left)
- 1 avocado, sliced
- 1 tomato, chopped
- 1 cup sour cream
- ½ cup thinly sliced radishes
- 4 seeded and sliced fresh jalapeño peppers

DIRECTIONS:

To make the beef filling, heat the oil in the skillet over medium. Add the onion and sauté for 3 minutes or until soft. Add the ground beef and cook, stirring to break up the meat, until it's no longer pink (about 4 minutes). Drain the liquid.

Add the garlic, chili powder, cumin, coriander, salt, and tomato sauce. Cook, stirring occasionally, over low heat for 10 minutes. (If the sauce is too thick, add a few tablespoons of water.)

Meanwhile, place your toppings in separate small bowls and set them on the table. Choose four or more toppings, depending on your family's tastes.

Place the tortillas, one at a time, in a large nonstick skillet over medium heat and warm for 1 minute, flipping once or twice, until soft. Place the warm tortillas in a basket and the beef filling in a bowl. Allow each person to layer ingredients into his or her own tortilla, then fold them up. Serves 4 to 6.

KIDS' STEPS: Kids can help prepare the toppings. Soft vegetables can be cut with plastic picnic knives, and other items, such as grated cheese and salsa, can simply be arranged in small bowls.

Prep time: 15 minutes Cooking time: 20 minutes

Family-size Hamburger

STUFFED WITH CHEESE, tomatoes, and pickles and served in wedge-shaped slices, this giant burger measures up in size and flavor — and family fun.

INGREDIENTS:

- 2 **pounds ground beef**
- 2 **tablespoons mustard**
- 2 **tablespoons Worcestershire sauce**
  Salt and pepper to taste
- ½ **pound cheese, sliced**
- 1 **tomato, sliced**
- 2 **to 3 thin slices red onion**
- ½ **cup pickle slices**
- ¼ **cup melted butter**
- 1 **tablespoon chili powder**
  Large round loaf of bread, sliced in half horizontally

DIRECTIONS:

Heat a grill or oven broiler. In a large bowl, mix together the ground beef, mustard, Worcestershire sauce, salt, and pepper. Shape the meat into an 11-inch patty and a 9-inch patty. Place the larger patty on a foil-covered pizza paddle or flat baking sheet. Layer on half of the cheese, the tomato, onion, and pickles. Add the remaining cheese, leaving a 2-inch margin around the edge. Top with the 9-inch patty and pinch together the edges of the two burgers. Combine the butter and chili powder and brush it on the burger.

Slide the burger off the paddle or baking sheet onto the grill or broiler pan (broil it 3 inches from the flame). Cook for 6 to 9 minutes on one side, then use the paddle or two spatulas to flip the burger. Brush on more butter and cook another 6 to 8 minutes or until it's done the way you like it. Place the burger between the bread "bun" and cut into 8 wedges. Serves 8.

KIDS' STEPS: Kids can measure and add ingredients to the beef mixture.

Prep time: 10 minutes   Cooking time: 15 minutes

The Better Burger

ONE OF THE SIMPLEST (and fastest) family dinners is the all-American hamburger. These burgers are nicely seasoned, and the added ketchup, mustard, and Worcestershire sauce help keep them moist. Serve with a salad and the Oven Baked Fries on page 79.

INGREDIENTS:

- 4 tablespoons ketchup
- 2 teaspoons Dijon mustard
- 4 teaspoons Worcestershire sauce
- 2 scallions, greens only, minced (optional)
- 2 pounds ground beef
- 8 hamburger rolls
  Toppings: ketchup, mayonnaise, salsa, steak sauce, pickles, cheese, mustard, lettuce, and onions

DIRECTIONS:

Stir the ketchup, mustard, Worcestershire sauce, and scallions (if desired) in a medium-size bowl. Add the beef and mix thoroughly. Form into patties or mini patties (see right).

Heat the grill or oven broiler to medium. Grill or broil the hamburgers for 12 minutes for medium or up to 18 for well-done, turning twice during the cooking time.

Right before the burgers are done, place the split buns, facedown, on the grill or under the broiler for a few seconds to warm and crisp them slightly. Fill the buns and set them on a platter next to the toppings. Serve immediately. Serves 6 to 8.

MINI BETTER BURGERS

For mini-sized burgers, pick up small dinner rolls from the baker's section of your supermarket. Shape the burger mixture into small patties. For medium, grill or broil the burgers for about 8 minutes; for well-done, grill for 10 minutes, turning once during the cooking time.

MY GREAT IDEA
Hearty Hamburgers

Love is rare — or better yet, in the case of the Aydinel family's valentine hamburgers, medium-well. A heart-shaped cookie cutter used on both the raw meat and the bun is all you need (for sanitation's sake, use it on the buns first). Suzy and Michael Aydinel's older kids — Christine, 6, and Michael, 4 (Suzy, 11 months, just watches), like to draw ketchup faces on their burgers before digging in.

KIDS' STEPS: Kids can mix the seasonings into the ground beef, then shape the patties (washing their hands immediately afterward).

Shepherd's Pie

KIDS JUST CAN'T get enough
of this classic hot and hearty
meat-and-potato pie. Served with
dinner rolls and a tossed salad, it's a
meal your child will be proud to have
helped prepare — and eager to eat.

INGREDIENTS:

  2 tablespoons butter
  1 large onion, chopped
  1 stalk celery, chopped
1¼ pounds ground beef
  1 garlic clove, minced
  2 tablespoons flour
  1 cup beef broth
  1 cup canned diced tomatoes or
     canned crushed tomatoes
     in puree
  1 teaspoon dried thyme

  ½ teaspoon dried rosemary
1½ cups cooked corn kernels
1½ teaspoons Worcestershire sauce
     Salt and pepper to taste
     Mashed Potato Clouds (see
     page 77)
  1 to 1½ cups grated white
     Cheddar cheese
     Paprika

DIRECTIONS:

Melt the butter in a large skillet over
medium heat. Sauté the onion and
celery in the butter, stirring often, for
about 5 to 6 minutes. Add the ground
beef to the pan and break it up with a
wooden spoon as it browns. Remove the
skillet from the stove and drain the fat.

    Put the skillet back on the burner
and set the heat to medium-low.
Stir the garlic and flour into the beef
mixture. Stir in the beef broth, then
the canned tomatoes, then the herbs,
corn, and Worcestershire sauce.
Gently simmer the mixture for several
minutes, partially covered, then add
salt (¼ teaspoon, give or take a little)
and pepper to taste.

    Transfer the mixture to a large
buttered casserole. Set the oven to
400°. Spoon the mashed potatoes
evenly over the filling. Sprinkle the
cheese over the top, then sprinkle
on some paprika. Bake the pie on the
center oven rack for about 20 minutes, until the top is golden brown.
Cool for several minutes before
serving, as the dish it is served in will
be very hot. Serves 5 to 6.

KIDS' STEPS: Kids can mash the
potatoes and sprinkle on the cheese.

Prep time: 15 minutes Cooking time: 35 minutes

Cheesy Meat Loaf

A S A WORKING MOTHER of three, *FamilyFun* recipe tester Amy Hamel often serves this meat loaf to her kids, who love its cheesy chunks.

INGREDIENTS:

- 1½ pounds lean ground beef
- ½ pound sweet pork sausage, casings removed
- 1 cup Cheddar cheese, cut into cubes
- 2 large eggs
- 1 medium-size onion, finely chopped
- ½ green bell pepper, seeded and finely chopped
- 1 teaspoon salt
- ½ teaspoon black pepper
- 1 teaspoon celery salt
- ½ teaspoon paprika
- 1 cup milk
- 1 cup fine dry bread crumbs

KIDS' STEPS: Kids can measure and mix the seasoning into the beef mixture.

DIRECTIONS:

Heat the oven to 350°. Line a large baking pan with greased aluminum foil and set it aside.

Combine all of the ingredients in a large mixing bowl. Using your hands, blend everything together until it is evenly mixed. Transfer the meat to the lined baking pan and form it into a long, fat loaf, about 10 inches by 5 inches. Bake the loaf for 60 to 70 minutes, until the center is cooked. (According to the USDA and the National Pork Board, pork should be cooked to medium doneness with an internal temperature of 160° before eating.) Serves 8.

FUN FOOD

Snowmen Sloppy Joes

For a silly supper on a chilly night, help your kids whip up these warm and tasty indoor snowmen.

First, prepare store-bought sloppy joe mix according to package directions. Next, arrange the bottom halves of three biscuits on a platter in the classic snowman formation. Spoon the sloppy joe mixture on top of each half, then top with the other biscuit half (hamburger buns also work well).

Have the kids make articles of clothing, facial features, and so on with the vegetables. We gave our snowmen fringed carrot scarves (made with a vegetable peeler and scissors), hats made from a mushroom slice and the top of a zucchini, scallion eyes, olive buttons, and red pepper mouths. Dig in while they're hot.

Prep time: 15 minutes Cooking time: 70 minutes

Pork on a Bun

WITH THE HELP of a slow
cooker, making this succulent
sandwich is a snap. In the morning,
place all the ingredients in your slow
cooker and dinner will be ready by
6:00. The final flavor will be deter-
mined largely by the brand of barbecue
sauce you select, so use a fresh bottle
and consider one that has a touch of
smoke flavor.

INGREDIENTS:
1   3- to 4-pound pork-butt
     roast or beef brisket
     Salt and pepper to taste

2   medium onions, sliced
1   16-ounce jar barbecue sauce
     Soft rolls

DIRECTIONS:
Carefully trim the meat of visible fat
and season it with salt and pepper.
Place the onions in the bottom of the
slow cooker, then lay the meat on
top of them. (You may have to cut the
brisket in half and stack the pieces.)
Pour about a half cup of the barbecue
sauce over the meat and turn to
coat. Cover and cook for 9 to 10 hours
on low.

Carefully remove the cooked meat
and pour out the fat and juices, re-
taining the onions. If you're using pork,
shred it with two forks. Put the pork
back in the cooker, mix in the remaining barbecue sauce, and let it cook
another half hour or so. (You could eat
it now, but it's better if it soaks awhile.)
If you're using beef brisket, slice the
meat across the grain and place it on a
platter, discarding any fat. Cover it with
sauce and let it sit for 10 minutes or so
— if you can bear it! Serve on soft
rolls, onions on the side. Serves 8 to 10.

KIDS' STEPS: Older kids can help
slice the onions. Younger kids
can pour the sauce into the cooker.

Prep time: 15 minutes   Cooking time: 10 hours

Zesty Ham and Pineapple

HAM STEAKS make for a quick dinner because they're precooked, so you essentially need only to heat them through. Jazz up your pan-fried, broiled, or grilled ham steak with our quick-to-mix mustard sauce.

INGREDIENTS:

- 4 tablespoons Dijon or creamy Dijon-style mustard
- 1 tablespoon maple syrup
- 1 tablespoon olive or vegetable oil
- ½ teaspoon 5-spice powder (or a mix of ⅛ teaspoon each of cinnamon, ground ginger, and ground cloves)
- 1 teaspoon soy sauce (optional)
  Ham steak (about 2 pounds and 1 inch thick)
  Canned pineapple slices

DIRECTIONS:
Whisk the mustard, maple syrup, oil, 5-spice powder, and soy sauce (if desired) in a small bowl. Cut the ham into individual portions and use a pastry brush to spread the mustard mixture on both sides of each piece. Pan-fry, broil, or grill the ham 5 or more minutes on each side until it heats through. Cook the pineapple slices at the same time and serve them atop the ham. Makes about 6 servings.

KID'S STEPS: Kids can brush the mustard sauce on the ham steaks.

FUN FOOD
Hot Dog Octopus

With a few simple cuts and a side of seaweed (aka spinach pasta), you can transform a plain hot dog into a fun dinner kids can't resist.

First, cook the pasta (we used fettuccine) according to the package directions. For the octopus, cut slits along the length of a hot dog, stopping about 1 inch from the end, to create 8 dangling arms. Boil the hot dog as directed on the package. Set the hot dog atop a bed of seaweed noodles and add a mustard or ketchup face before serving.

Back-to-Basics London Broil

DRESS UP THE classic dinner steak with one of our accompanying sauces. For a true back-to-basics dinner, support your town butcher — you'll often get the best cut of beef while contributing to an important local trade.

INGREDIENTS:
2 pounds London broil or flank steak, 1 inch thick
Coarse salt and black pepper
Vegetable oil

DIRECTIONS:
Heat your oven broiler or grill. Grease the broiling pan or grill before laying on the steaks. Rub the meat with the coarse salt and a bit of pepper. Cook 3 inches from the flame for 4 to 6 minutes per side for medium. To serve, slice the meat on the diagonal, following the grain. Serves 4 to 6.

DIJON-HERB BUTTER
In a food processor or by hand, mix 6 tablespoons butter with 2 tablespoons mustard and 1 minced shallot. Add 8 chopped sprigs of parsley and 8 chopped chives. Pat into a log on waxed paper, refrigerate, and slice into rounds. Dot on warm steak.

LEMON PEPPER
Before you cook the steak, coat both sides with store-bought lemon pepper.

VEGGIE SMOTHER
Sauté 8 ounces of sliced mushrooms, 1 medium-size chopped onion, 1 sliced green pepper, and 1 crushed garlic clove in 1 tablespoon of butter or olive oil. Spoon over the warm steak just before serving.

PARSLEY PESTO
In a food processor, blend 2 cups fresh parsley, 1 crushed garlic clove, and 2 tablespoons sunflower seeds with ⅓ cup olive oil. Add 3 tablespoons Parmesan cheese and ½ teaspoon salt. Dot on warm steak.

HORSERADISH DIPPING SAUCE
Mix ½ cup sour cream with ¼ cup prepared horseradish and a dash of Worcestershire sauce.

LAST-MINUTE MARINADE
Marinate the steak in Garden Green Salad Dressing (page 8) or any Italian salad dressing for at least 1 hour before cooking.

KIDS' STEPS: Kids can help mix up one of the sauces for the steak.

Prep time: 15 minutes Cooking time: 12 minutes

Steak Stir-fry

THIS SIMPLE, SAUCY stir-fry is a snap to make and goes great with the Chinese Fried Rice on page 74.

INGREDIENTS:

- 2 tablespoons soy sauce
- 1 tablespoon rice wine vinegar
- 1 tablespoon sugar
- ½ teaspoon sesame oil
- 2½ teaspoons cornstarch
- 1 garlic clove, minced
- 1 teaspoon minced fresh ginger
- ¾ pound flank steak
- 2 tablespoons vegetable oil
- 8 ounces pea pods, trimmed
- 1 medium red bell pepper, cut into ¼-inch-wide strips
- ½ cup chicken broth
- 2 tablespoons oyster-flavored sauce

DIRECTIONS:

Make the marinade for the meat by measuring the soy sauce, rice wine vinegar, sugar, and sesame oil into a medium-size bowl. Add the cornstarch and blend it in with the back of a spoon. Stir in the garlic and ginger.

Trim any fat or gristle from the steak. Cut into pieces about 1½ inches long and not quite ¼ inch thick. Stir the meat into the marinade. Cover and set it aside for 30 minutes to marinate.

Heat a wok or large sauté pan. If you're using a wok, drizzle the 2 tablespoons of oil around the inside near the top (it will run down and coat the sides sufficiently). Otherwise, gently rotate the pan to evenly spread the oil. Add the meat, spreading it out in the pan, and stir-fry it for 2 to 3 minutes or

until it is well browned. Use a slotted spoon to transfer the cooked meat to a plate. Immediately add the pea pods, pepper, and chicken broth to the pan. Cook, uncovered, over high heat 1 to 3 minutes stirring occasionally. Stir in the meat and oyster sauce. Cook for another minute or two, until the vegetables are tender. Serves 4.

KIDS' STEPS: Kids can mix the meat pieces in the marinade.

TIP: Cut beef across the grain for thin, neat slicing. Use a sharp knife and a sawing motion (instead of pushing down on the blade).

Prep time: 20 minutes   Marinating time: 30 minutes   Cooking time: 8 minutes

Grilled Sirloin Kebabs
with Ginger-pineapple Marinade

TANGY AND GINGERY, this recipe wins raves from kids and grown-ups alike. The meat marinates in advance, so you can grill up a summery supper fast.

INGREDIENTS:

 5 garlic cloves, crushed
 2 tablespoons finely chopped
    fresh ginger
 ½ cup low-salt soy sauce
 ¼ cup olive oil
 1 tablespoon sugar
 1 cup pineapple juice
 1 teaspoon black pepper
 2 pounds sirloin steak,
    cut into cubes

DIRECTIONS:

First, prepare the marinade. In a medium-size bowl, whisk together the garlic, ginger, soy sauce, olive oil, sugar, pineapple juice, and black pepper.

To make the kebabs, pierce each side of the beef cubes several times with a sharp knife (this allows the marinade to penetrate). Add the beef to the bowl of marinade and stir to coat well. Marinate in the refrigerator overnight (or at least 8 hours), turning occasionally.

When you are ready to grill, skewer the meat, then barbecue the kebabs over medium heat for 4 to 7 minutes per side (medium rare). Serves 6.

KIDS' STEPS: Younger kids can whisk the marinade ingredients. Older kids can skewer the veggies.

Prep time: 10 minutes   Cooking time: 12 minutes   Marinating time: 8 hours

Peachy Sweet Shish Kebab

THIS FLAVORFUL marinade works well not only with lamb but also with extra-firm tofu, chicken, and beef. After tasting this recipe, you may find it becomes a staple at your family cookouts.

INGREDIENTS:

- 1 cup fresh mint leaves, rinsed and lightly packed
- 1 small jalapeño pepper, sliced in half and seeds removed (optional)
- 1-inch piece fresh ginger, peeled and cut in two
- 2 garlic cloves, peeled
- 8 tablespoons peach jam
- 1 tablespoon soy sauce
- ¼ cup water
- 2 pounds lamb shish kebab cubes, trimmed of fat

DIRECTIONS:

Place the mint, optional jalapeño pepper, ginger, garlic, jam, soy sauce, and water in a food processor and process until blended. The sauce should be thick but pourable; add more water if needed. Reserve a portion of the marinade for basting and transfer the rest to a gallon-size sealable bag, add the lamb cubes, seal, and gently shake to cover all the pieces. Refrigerate for 24 hours, turning occasionally.

Remove the lamb from the marinade and thread onto skewers (metal or bamboo previously soaked in water, see right). Grill for about 5 to 7 minutes for medium (pink inside), brushing occasionally with the reserved marinade. Serve with grilled peppers, onions, and tomatoes, skewered and cooked separately to avoid burning. Serves 4.

KIDS' STEPS: Kids can press the buttons on the food processor and add the lamb cubes to the bag of marinade.

COOKING TIPS
Grilling Hints

- For charcoal grills, invest in an inexpensive chimney starter, which makes starting your fire a snap.

- Soak wooden skewers for kebabs in water for 30 minutes prior to piercing meats and vegetables to prevent burning.

- Before cooking, always heat the grill rack for 5 minutes over coals.

- Brush on thick or sweet sauces during the last 5 minutes of grilling to prevent burning.

- Try not to pierce meat often, as juices will be lost.

- Use a wire brush to clean the grill after cooking sessions.

- And don't forget long-handled tools, such as tongs and a brush for spreading sauces.

**Prep time: 15 minutes   Marinating time: 24 hours
Cooking time: 7 minutes**

Slow Cooker Basics

- For the best cooking results, make sure your cooker is between half and three-quarters full.

- The delicious aromas wafting from your slow cooker may tempt you to take a peek inside, but don't unless the recipe instructs you to. It takes about 20 minutes for the cooker to regain that lost heat, which means a longer wait.

- Don't be surprised by the small amount of liquid in most slow cooker recipes. Liquids don't evaporate from the slow cooker as they do in traditional stove-top methods.

- When a slow-cooker recipe calls for chicken, try chicken thighs. Thighs stay juicy and tender, while chicken breasts can become tough and stringy.

- Vegetables take longer to cook than meat. For the best taste and texture, slice them and place them in the bottom of the cooker under the meat, where they'll be closer to the heat source.

Best-ever Beef Stew

THERE IS PERHAPS no better way to prepare a beef stew than with a long, slow simmer. The low heat and moisture slowly break down the structure of the muscle tissue, tenderizing the meat. But thanks to the slow cooker, you won't need to stay at home while the stew takes its time cooking. Just let it simmer all day long.

INGREDIENTS:

- 1 large onion, halved and thinly sliced
- 2 medium carrots, peeled and thinly sliced
- 2 large potatoes, cut into ½-inch chunks
- 1 to 1½ cups peeled and diced rutabaga (about half a small rutabaga)
- 1 cup fresh green beans, in bite-size pieces
- 1 pound beef stew-meat chunks
- 1 bay leaf
- ½ teaspoon dried thyme
- 1 garlic clove, crushed
- 3 cups beef stock
- 2 tablespoons light brown sugar
- ¾ teaspoon salt
- 2 teaspoons Worcestershire sauce

Pepper to taste
- 3 tablespoons all-purpose flour
- 2 teaspoons tomato paste

DIRECTIONS:

Place all the ingredients except the flour and the tomato paste in a slow cooker; stir to combine. Cover and cook on the low setting for 8 to 9 hours or on high for 4 to 5, until the beef is tender and the potatoes are just fork-tender. Stir the stew once or twice as it cooks, if possible.

About 30 minutes before serving, transfer a ladleful of the broth to a small mixing bowl. Add the flour and tomato paste and whisk until smooth. Stir the mixture into the stew and cook for the remaining half hour. Serves 6 to 8.

VARIATION Like so many slow-cooker dishes, this one readily accepts additions and adjustments. You may use a cup of dry red wine in place of the beef stock or add a handful of dry lentils, perhaps ⅓ cup, at the outset. If you like, you can use a sliced parsnip, too. There are plenty of ways to play with the basic formula.

KIDS' STEPS: Kids can cut the beans into bite-size pieces, crush the garlic in a garlic press, and measure ingredients into the slow cooker.

Prep time: 20 minutes Cooking time: Up to 9 hours

Plain and Simple Roast Chicken

ON A LEISURELY Sunday afternoon, pop a roasting chicken in the oven and it will be finished by dinnertime. Then your family can sit down to an old-fashioned dinner together. This recipe welcomes embellishments, such as the ones at right.

INGREDIENTS:

- 1 4- to 5-pound roasting chicken
   Half a lemon
- 1 large onion, sliced
- 2 tablespoons olive oil
- 1 teaspoon thyme
- ½ teaspoon coarse salt
- ¼ teaspoon pepper

DIRECTIONS:

Preheat the oven to 400°. Remove the giblets, thoroughly rinse the chicken, and pat dry. Squeeze the juice from the lemon half over the chicken, then stuff the half into the cavity. Close the cavity with small skewers and tie the legs together with string.

Make a bed of onion slices in the bottom of a roasting pan and place the chicken, breast side up, on the onions. Drizzle with the olive oil, sprinkle with the thyme, salt, and pepper and bake for 1¼ to 1½ hours, basting frequently, until the juices from behind the leg run clear. Let rest 5 minutes, then carve. Serves 4 to 6.

VEGGIE ROAST CHICKEN
Surround the chicken with peeled carrots and pearl onions, unpeeled new potatoes, and whole mushrooms. Serve with the roasted vegetables on the side.

ORANGE-GINGER CHICKEN
Arrange orange slices on the bird, pour ½ cup orange juice over the top, and sprinkle with 1 tablespoon of peeled and minced fresh ginger.

APPLE-HAZELNUT CHICKEN
Place cored apple halves and peeled pearl onions in the roasting pan. Arrange apple slices on the bird and add a dash of cinnamon. Drizzle apple brandy over the bird for a fuller flavor. Ten minutes before the chicken is done, add 1 cup hazelnuts to the pan.

LEMON-ROSEMARY CHICKEN
Place lemon slices on the chicken and sprinkle generously with rosemary and a little olive oil.

STUFFED CHICKEN
Just before roasting, loosely stuff the chicken with your favorite stuffing mix. Increase the cooking time by 25 minutes.

KIDS' STEPS: Kids can arrange the vegetables in the roasting pan and help tie the chicken legs together with string.

Prep time: 15 minutes Cooking time: 1¹/₂ hours

Mu Shu Chicken Wraps

FAMILYFUN EDITORIAL researcher Ellen Harter Wall got her first slow cooker a dozen years ago, but she and her husband, Chris, became die-hard fans only after their kids were born and she started working noon to five at her local library. These wraps are a family favorite.

INGREDIENTS:

1 onion, diced
1½ to 2 pounds boneless, skinless chicken thighs
Salt and pepper to taste
1 cup hoisin sauce
2 tablespoons honey
¼ teaspoon ground ginger
1 12-ounce bag broccoli coleslaw mix (such as Mann's brand) or other toppings
Flour tortillas or flatbread

DIRECTIONS:
Place the diced onion in the slow cooker. Season the chicken with salt and pepper, place it on top of the onions, and cook on low for 4 to 5 hours, or until the meat pulls apart easily with a fork. With a slotted spoon, transfer the chicken and onions to a medium bowl and shred the meat.

In a small bowl, mix together the hoisin sauce, honey, and ginger, then stir the mixture into the shredded chicken and onion. Place a small handful of broccoli coleslaw on a warm tortilla, add several spoonfuls of the chicken mixture, and roll up. Makes 6 to 8 rolls.

KIDS' STEPS: Kids can layer their tortilla with the broccoli coleslaw and chicken mixture.

Prep time: 10 minutes Cooking time: 4 to 5 hours

Chicken Fajitas

I T SEEMS THAT anything wrapped in a tortilla is a smash hit with kids. Set out this seasoned grilled chicken and assorted toppings and let the family custom-make their own fajitas. For kids who don't like cooked green peppers, serve them raw in a bowl with the other toppings.

INGREDIENTS:

- 1 ripe avocado, cut into chunks and tossed in l teaspoon lime juice (or Creamy Guacamole, see page 24)
  Salsa
  Sour cream
  Fresh cilantro, chopped
- 4 teaspoons ground cumin
- 4 teaspoons chili powder
- 1 teaspoon dried oregano
- ½ teaspoon salt
- 2 boneless, skinless chicken breasts, cut in half
- 1 small red, yellow, or green pepper, sliced
- 1 onion, sliced
- 2 teaspoons olive oil
- 4 8-inch flour tortillas

DIRECTIONS:

First, place your toppings (avocado or guacamole, salsa, sour cream, and cilantro) in separate bowls and set them on your kitchen table.

Next, make the chicken rub. Combine the cumin, chili powder, oregano, and salt in a shallow bowl. Lightly rub the spices into the chicken with your fingertips until the meat is coated on all sides.

Heat your grill to medium. Grill the chicken on both sides, just until cooked through, about 8 minutes. Remove from the heat, slice thinly, and set the chicken on a serving platter.

While the chicken is cooking, toss the sliced pepper and onion in the olive oil. Set them on the grill, using a vegetable screen if desired, and cook for 5 to 8 minutes, turning once. Remove from the heat and set on the platter with the chicken.

Place the tortillas on the grill for 5 to 7 seconds on each side, turning with tongs, until hot. Set out the grilled chicken, pepper, and onion with the toppings and tortillas. Let everyone assemble and roll their own fajitas. Serves 4.

KIDS' STEPS: Kids can set toppings in bowls and rub the spices into the chicken (washing hands thoroughly afterward).

LEFTOVER IDEA
Chicken Quesadilla

Using leftover seasoned chicken from the fajita recipe at left, you and your kids can cook up this crispy quesadilla in a flash.

For each quesadilla, use a pastry brush to coat one side of a tortilla with oil. Place the tortilla, oiled side down, on a large plate. On half of the tortilla, layer Monterey Jack cheese, the seasoned chicken, and any other items that your family likes, such as black beans, corn, or salsa. Fold the tortilla in half and transfer to a skillet.

Cook over medium heat for about 1 minute. Flip and cook for another minute or two, until the cheese melts and the tortilla is golden brown.

Whether you serve the quesadillas whole or cut them into wedges, eat right away (they taste best fresh). Serve with guacamole, sour cream, and salsa.

Prep time: 20 minutes Cooking time: 16 minutes

Chicken Tenders

THESE CHICKEN TENDERS, which are coated with mashed potato flakes, turn out textured and crispy on the outside, with only as much spice as you (and your family) like. And because they're baked instead of fried, they're a healthy alternative to the fast-food kind. Serve with a side of the extra instant mashed potatoes and a salad.

INGREDIENTS:

1   tablespoon canola oil
    About 1½ pounds chicken tenders (raw)
1   cup unbleached white flour
1   cup mashed potato flakes (we used Idaho Spuds)
1   teaspoon creole or Cajun seasoning mix (optional)
1   teaspoon salt
1   teaspoon pepper
2   teaspoons ground oregano
1   teaspoon garlic powder
¾   cup low-fat buttermilk (or regular milk)
1   large egg
    Canola cooking spray (see A Note on Cooking Spray, page 72)

DIRECTIONS:

Heat the oven to 450°. Evenly coat a baking sheet with the tablespoon of canola oil. Rinse the chicken tenders, then pat them dry with paper towels and set aside.

In a medium bowl, add the flour, mashed potato flakes, seasoning mix (if desired), salt, pepper, oregano, and garlic powder and stir to blend well. Add the buttermilk and egg in another medium bowl and beat with a fork or mixer until smooth.

Dip each tender first in the flour mixture, then in the egg mixture, then back in the flour mixture. Place the coated pieces on the prepared sheet and let them sit for 10 to 15 minutes. Before baking, spray the tops generously with canola cooking spray.

Bake the chicken until the thickest part is cooked through and the coating is golden brown, 15 to 20 minutes, flipping after 10 minutes. Serves 4 to 6.

KIDS' STEPS: Kids can mix up the chicken coating, crack the egg, and dip the tenders in the mixtures.

Prep time: 15 minutes   Cooking time: 20 minutes

Apricot Drumsticks

THIS YUMMY RECIPE should pass the taste test of even the most finicky eaters. The chicken is baked in a sauce of apricot preserves, ginger, and garlic. Serve with rice and peas.

INGREDIENTS:

2 pounds chicken drumsticks
1 tablespoon peanut oil
1 12-ounce jar apricot preserves
2 tablespoons peeled and minced fresh ginger root
2 garlic cloves, crushed
½ cup canned low-salt chicken broth

DIRECTIONS:
Heat the oven to 350°. Rinse the chicken and remove the skin, if desired. In a nonstick skillet, heat the peanut oil over medium-high. Brown the chicken on all sides. Remove from the pan and place on a paper towel.

Place the chicken in a 9- by 13- by 2-inch baking dish. In a small bowl, mix the preserves, ginger, garlic, and chicken broth, then pour over the chicken.

Bake, uncovered, for 15 minutes or until the juices run clear and there

are no traces of pink in the center. Serves 4.

KIDS' STEPS: Kids can mix the apricot sauce and pour it over the chicken.

Prep time: 20 minutes Cooking time: 15 minutes

Cracker Chicken

COATED WITH a homemade "shake and bake" mix made from crackers and seasonings, this oven-baked chicken tastes as good as fried chicken. It can be served warm or at room temperature (so it's great for a school potluck).

INGREDIENTS:

- 24 butter crackers, such as Ritz
- ¼ cup grated Parmesan cheese
- ½ teaspoon paprika
- ¼ teaspoon garlic powder
- ¼ teaspoon salt
- ¼ teaspoon black pepper
- 10 small, skinned chicken drumsticks or about 1½ pounds boneless, skinless chicken breasts cut into 1-inch-wide strips
- 2 large eggs
- 2 tablespoons honey
- 1 tablespoon water

DIRECTIONS:

Heat the oven to 400°. Combine the crackers, Parmesan cheese, paprika, garlic powder, salt, and pepper in a food processor and process until the mixture resembles coarse meal. (If you don't have a food processor, you can crush the crackers in a sealable plastic bag, using a rolling pin.) Transfer the mixture to a shallow bowl or a sheet of waxed paper.

Rinse the chicken with cold water and pat dry with paper towels. In a shallow bowl, beat the eggs, honey, and water until blended. Dip the drumsticks or breast pieces into the egg mixture, then dredge them in the cracker mixture. Place the pieces on a lightly oiled baking sheet.

Bake drumsticks for 15 minutes, then turn them over and bake for 20 minutes more, or until the chicken is tender and the coating golden. Bake chicken strips for 16 to 20 minutes, turning once. Serves 8 to 10.

CORNFLAKE CHICKEN

For an even crunchier skin, use 3 cups of crushed cornflakes instead of crackers. Add ¼ teaspoon ground sage to the mix and follow the coating and cooking instructions above.

DIPPING SAUCE

A touch of ginger and cinnamon give this quick-to-mix sauce a tasty tang. In a small bowl, mix ½ cup ketchup, 2 tablespoons maple syrup, 1 tablespoon soy sauce, ½ teaspoon cinnamon, ¼ teaspoon ground ginger, and a dash hot pepper sauce (optional) until well blended. Cover and refrigerate until ready to use. Makes about ¾ cup.

BREADS WE LOVE
Easy Biscuits

The trick to making good biscuits is handling the dough as little as possible. First, heat the oven to 400°. In a big bowl, mix together 2 cups of all-purpose flour, 1 tablespoon of baking powder, 1 tablespoon of sugar, and ½ teaspoon of salt. Using your fingers, work in 5 tablespoons of softened butter, until it has the consistency of cornmeal. Then stir in ⅔ cup of milk.

Turn the biscuit dough onto a floured surface and roll it out to about a ½-inch thickness. Use a cookie cutter to shape the biscuits. Place them on a greased baking sheet and bake for 10 to 12 minutes or until light brown. Makes about 10 biscuits.

KIDS' STEPS: Kids can crush the crackers in a bag. They can also mix up the coating, then dip the chicken in it and cover it thoroughly.

TIP: To test chicken for doneness, slice into the center of the thickest part of the piece down to the bone. If the juice runs clear and the meat is no longer pink, it's done.

Prep time: 15 minutes   Cooking time: 35 minutes

Sweet-and-sour Grilled Chicken

I T ' S   A   S N A P to make this chicken dish, and kids love its sweet flavor. Reserve some sauce for drizzling over the cooked meat or for dipping. The leftovers can be sliced and topped on a tossed salad.

INGREDIENTS:

- 2 garlic cloves, crushed
- 2 tablespoons balsamic vinegar
  Juice of ½ lime
  Juice of ½ lemon
- ⅓ cup light brown sugar
- 2 tablespoons Dijon mustard
- ⅓ cup honey
- 1 teaspoon salt
- ½ teaspoon black pepper
- 4 tablespoons olive oil
- 2 whole boneless, skinless chicken breasts, cut in half
  Italian parsley (optional)

DIRECTIONS:

In a shallow bowl, whisk together the garlic, vinegar, lime and lemon juices, brown sugar, mustard, honey, and salt and pepper. Whisk in the olive oil.

Divide the sauce into thirds. Reserve one portion of the mixture for basting and one for dipping sauce, then add the chicken to the dish with the remaining portion and turn it to coat.

Grill the chicken for 4 to 5 minutes per side, or until the juices run clear. During the last minutes of cooking, baste the chicken with the portion of the reserved sauce to glaze it. Garnish with the chopped Italian parsley, if desired. Serve with the other reserved portion of the marinade for dipping. Serves 4.

KIDS' STEPS: Younger kids can whisk the marinade ingredients and pour the sauce over the chicken.

Prep time: 10 minutes   Cooking time: 10 minutes

Chicken Yogurt Kebabs

A YOGURT MARINADE makes these chicken kebabs moist. They taste great sprinkled with a little hot sauce (we recommend Choalula brand) or a squeeze of lemon. While you have the grill going, cook up some Veggie Kebabs to serve alongside the chicken (see below).

INGREDIENTS:

- ⅔ cup plain low-fat yogurt
- 2 teaspoons brown sugar
- 2 teaspoons hot sauce, plus extra to eat with the chicken
- 1 teaspoon ground cumin
- 2 garlic cloves, minced
- ¼ teaspoon salt
- 8 boneless chicken breast halves
- Lemon wedges (optional)

DIRECTIONS:

Combine a few tablespoons of the yogurt with the brown sugar in a medium-size bowl and mix until well blended. Add the remaining yogurt, hot sauce, cumin, garlic, and salt.

Cut each chicken breast half into 6 to 8 equal pieces. Add to the yogurt mixture and stir until well combined. Thread the chicken onto eight skewers. Place in a doubled gallon-size sealable plastic bag (to guard against leaks). Chill for 30 minutes to 2 hours.

Grill the kebabs over medium heat, rotating sides every few minutes, until cooked through, about 10 to 14 minutes total. Serve with extra hot sauce and lemon wedges. Serves 6 to 8.

VEGGIE KEBAB

Thread cherry tomatoes, zucchini, onion, and other vegetables on skewers, brush with olive oil, and grill until slightly tender.

KIDS' STEPS: Kids can help measure the ingredients and mix up the yogurt marinade.

QUICK HIT
Easy Dry Rub

This easy dry rub makes your grilled chicken simply mouthwatering and forms a nice crust during grilling. Make a batch of the spicy powder, store it in your cupboard, and use it all summer long to give your chicken zing.

- 1 tablespoon black pepper
- 2 tablespoons cumin
- 2 tablespoons chili powder
- 2 tablespoons brown sugar
- 1 tablespoon white sugar
- 1 tablespoon oregano
- 4 tablespoons paprika
- 2 tablespoons salt
- 3 tablespoons garlic powder
- 1 tablespoon celery salt

Pour all of the spices into a sandwich-size sealable plastic bag. Shake well. This mix can be stored at room temperature in the sealed bag for months — and it makes enough rub to cover approximately 5½ pounds of chicken.

Prep time: 15 minutes Marinating time: 2 hours Cooking time: 15 minutes

Turkey Pilaf

CLEANUP IS a breeze with this one-skillet dish. It begins with a boxed rice mix, then gets dressed up with raisins, pine nuts, and spinach.

INGREDIENTS:
- 1 onion, peeled and chopped
- 3 carrots, peeled and chopped
- 2 cups fresh spinach (3 handfuls)
- 1¼ pounds ground turkey
- 2½ cups water
- 1 6-ounce package rice pilaf mix
- 2 tablespoons butter or margarine
- 1 cup raisins
- ¾ cup pine nuts

DIRECTIONS:
Peel and chop the onion and carrots. Rinse the spinach, remove the stems, and tear it into bite-size pieces.

In a saucepan, over medium-high heat, brown the turkey, stirring to break up the meat, for about 5 minutes, or until it begins to brown. Pour off any liquid. Add the chopped onion and carrots and cook for 3 more minutes.

Add the water, rice mix, and butter or margarine, and stir well. Add the raisins, pine nuts, and spinach. Cover and simmer over low, stirring occasionally, for 25 minutes. Serves 6.

KIDS' STEPS: Kids can rinse and tear the spinach and measure the raisins and nuts.

Prep time: 10 minutes Cooking time: 33 minutes

White Turkey and Corn Stew

Cook up a pot of this zesty stew, made with leftover roasted turkey and flavored with cumin and chili powder.

INGREDIENTS:

- 1 tablespoon vegetable oil
- 1½ cups chopped onion
- 2 garlic cloves, crushed
- 4 cups cooked white turkey meat, diced
- 1 tablespoon ground cumin
- 1½ teaspoons chili powder
- 1 teaspoon mild jalapeño sauce
- ½ teaspoon salt
- 2½ cups chicken broth
- 1 10-ounce box frozen corn
- 1 15.5-ounce can white beans, drained and rinsed
- 1 4-ounce can diced green chilies, drained
- ½ cup sour cream
- ¼ cup chopped fresh cilantro

DIRECTIONS:

Heat the oil in a 4-quart, heavy-bottomed pot, add the onion, and cook for 1 to 2 minutes or until soft. Add the garlic and continue cooking for 30 seconds. Add the turkey, cumin, chili powder, jalapeño sauce, salt, and chicken broth. Mix well. Bring to a boil, then reduce to a simmer.

Stir in the corn, beans, and chilies and cook until heated through. Remove from the heat and stir in the sour cream and cilantro. Serves 6 to 8.

KIDS' STEPS: Kids can crush the garlic in a garlic press, and wash and snip the cilantro with scissors.

Prep time: 15 minutes Cooking time: 15 minutes

LEFTOVER IDEA
Turkey Sandwiches

For a quick and healthy dinner, serve your family one of these gourmet turkey sandwiches. You can use leftover roasted turkey or sliced turkey from a deli.

THE CAESAR WRAP

Sliced turkey, shredded romaine, diced tomatoes, shredded Parmesan cheese, and creamy Caesar dressing rolled in a flour tortilla.

TURKEY PARMIGIANA

Thick-sliced roasted turkey topped with spaghetti sauce and shredded mozzarella, broiled on crusty Italian bread.

TURKEY REUBEN

Sliced turkey topped with sauerkraut, Thousand Island dressing, and Swiss cheese, on grilled rye bread.

TURKEY BLT

Sliced turkey, bacon, lettuce, tomato, and mayonnaise on toast.

THE CALIFORNIA ROLL-UP

Large flour tortilla stuffed with sliced turkey, lettuce, tomato, avocado, alfalfa sprouts, and shredded Jack cheese.

Tex-Mex Turkey Tacos

FOR A FAMILIAR yet surprising meal, fill a taco shell with this mildly spicy turkey meat and let your kids pile it high with their favorite toppings. The filling can also be used for nachos, quesadillas, and burritos.

INGREDIENTS:

- 1 tablespoon vegetable oil
- ½ cup chopped onion
- 1 8-ounce can tomato sauce
- ½ cup water
- 2 tablespoons chili powder
- 1 teaspoon ground cumin
- ½ teaspoon salt
- 3 cups shredded cooked turkey meat (to shred the turkey, use a fork to pull it apart against the grain)
- 12 taco shells

TOPPINGS:

- ¾ cup shredded Cheddar cheese
  Chopped lettuce
  Chopped tomatoes
  Chopped avocado
  Sliced olives

DIRECTIONS:

Heat the oil over medium heat in a large skillet. Add the onion and cook for 1 to 2 minutes. Add the tomato sauce, water, chili powder, cumin, and salt. Bring to a boil, then reduce to a simmer and cook for 2 to 3 minutes. Stir in the turkey and cook until heated through.

Place ¼ cup of the taco filling in each taco shell. Top with 1 tablespoon of shredded Cheddar, lettuce, tomatoes, avocado, and olives. Serves 6.

KIDS' STEPS: Kids can pull apart the pieces of cooked turkey to shred it. Older kids can chop the lettuce, tomatoes, and avocado.

Prep time: 15 minutes Cooking time: 10 minutes

Mini Turkey Cheeseburgers

GROUND TURKEY CAN be dry when it's overcooked, but the couscous in this recipe keeps these burgers remarkably moist. The mini burgers are cute (and sometimes less sloppy), but if you prefer grown-up-size burgers, this recipe makes four, each served in a pita half. While you have the box of couscous open, mix up extras and serve as a side dish.

INGREDIENTS:

- ⅓ cup water
- ¼ cup dry couscous
- 12 ounces ground turkey
- 1 tablespoon grainy mustard
- 1 tablespoon ketchup
- 1 tablespoon Worcestershire sauce
- 1 small garlic clove, minced
- ¼ teaspoon pepper
- 1 cup grated Cheddar or your favorite cheese
- 4 6-inch pitas, each cut into quarters
- Ketchup, mustard, and pickles to taste (optional)
- 5 lettuce leaves, washed and dried and torn into little pieces (optional)

DIRECTIONS:

Bring the water to a boil in a small pan. Pour it into a medium-size bowl, add the couscous, and cover. Let it sit until most of the water is absorbed. Uncover, then let the couscous cool, about 10 to 15 minutes. Add the turkey, mustard, ketchup, Worcestershire sauce, garlic, and pepper, and mix well. Divide the mixture equally into 16 balls, each about 1½ inches. Flatten into 1-inch-thick mini patties.

Grill, broil, or panfry the patties over medium heat for 6 to 8 minutes, or until the meat is just cooked through, turning once halfway through cooking. If grilling the mini patties, do so on a vegetable rack placed on an uncovered grill (so there's no danger of their falling into the coals).

Sprinkle each burger with cheese and cover until cheese is melted. Remove the burgers and stuff each into a pita triangle. Set out ketchup, mustard, pickles, and lettuce for toppings. Makes 16 baby burgers and serves 6 to 8.

MY GREAT IDEA
What's Cooking?

"Each summer when the kids were young, we designated Friday as children's cooking night. When Brian was twelve and Dawn, nine, I began letting them plan dinner and dessert on alternating weeks. They chose the menu, shopped (I gave them a $10 limit), cooked, and made or bought dessert. Some weeks, we sat down to a candlelight dinner, and others, we sent out for pizza. I was surprised at the ideas they came up with and what they could accomplish in the kitchen."

—Dorris Creter
Sarasota, Florida

KIDS' STEPS: Kids can measure the couscous, mustard, ketchup, and Worcestershire sauce and stuff the burgers into the pita triangle.

Prep time: 15 minutes Cooking time: 25 minutes

Friendly Fish Filets

INSTEAD OF BEING deep-fried, these flaky, golden fish filets are coated with crackers and panfried in a small amount of canola oil. Serve them plain or create a fish sandwich with a hamburger bun, a slice of Cheddar cheese, lettuce, and a small dollop of Homemade Tartar Sauce (see recipe on page 53).

INGREDIENTS:

    ¾ pound white fish (such as
        grouper or cod)
    ¾ cup all-purpose flour
    ½ cup buttermilk
    ¾ cup crumbs from wheat
        crackers (such as
        Wheatsworth), preferably
        low-sodium and low-fat,
        ground in a food processor
        or crushed with a rolling pin
    ½ teaspoon salt
    ½ teaspoon pepper
    ¼ teaspoon garlic powder
    1 tablespoon finely chopped
        fresh parsley
    1½ tablespoons canola oil

DIRECTIONS:

Cut the filets into 4 squares, each about 3½ by 3½ inches, rinse them, and dry well on a paper towel.

In a small bowl, add the flour. Pour the buttermilk into another small bowl. Combine the wheat-cracker crumbs, salt, pepper, garlic powder, and fresh parsley in a medium, shallow bowl and blend well with a whisk. Dip each fish square into the flour, then the buttermilk, then the cracker crumb mixture. Set the pieces aside and heat a medium nonstick frying pan over medium-high heat.

Pour canola oil into the frying pan, then put in all 4 fish squares. Fry the fish until the bottoms are golden brown, about 4 minutes, then flip over the fish to brown the other side, about 3 minutes more. If you're making sandwiches, turn off the heat, lay the cheese slices over the hot fish squares, and cover the pan for a minute to melt the cheese. Serves 4.

KIDS' STEPS: Kids can crush the crackers and coat the fish in the cracker coating.

Prep time: 30 minutes   Cooking time: 10 minutes

Shrimp on a Stick

THIS UNBELIEVABLY EASY recipe brings the fun of popcorn shrimp to your own backyard grill. Ideal as either an appetizer or a main course, the shrimp is smothered in bread crumbs and garlic, then grilled golden brown and topped with fresh lemon juice. Traditional cocktail sauce and store-bought sesame-ginger sauce are both great for dipping.

INGREDIENTS:

- 1 pound uncooked medium shrimp
- ¼ cup olive oil
- 2 garlic cloves, finely chopped
- ½ cup seasoned bread crumbs
- ½ lemon
  Salt and pepper to taste

DIRECTIONS:

Peel, devein, and rinse the shrimp, then place them in a bowl with the olive oil and garlic. Add the bread crumbs and toss until the shrimp are evenly coated.

Thread the shrimp onto skewers, then grill them over medium heat for about 2 minutes per side, or until they are opaque in the center and the crumb coating begins to brown. Transfer them to a platter and remove the skewers. Squeeze on some lemon juice and add salt and pepper to taste. Serve plain or with dipping sauce. Serves 8 as an appetizer or 4 as a main course.

KIDS' STEPS: Kids can help by tossing the shrimp in the bread crumbs.

QUICK SAUCE

Homemade Tartar Sauce

Crown your fish filet with a wholesome homemade topping.

- ¼ cup mayonnaise
- ¼ cup fat-free or light sour cream
- 1 tablespoon sweet pickle relish
- 1 tablespoon finely chopped onion
- 1 tablespoon finely chopped fresh parsley

Whisk all ingredients together in a small bowl. Add pepper to taste. Cover and chill until needed. Makes about ⅔ cup of tartar sauce.

Prep time: 15 minutes Grilling time: 7 minutes

QUICK SAUCE
Mango Salsa

Spanish for "sauce," salsa comes in many varieties, including this sweet version that gives broiled fish (or chicken or corn chips) extra zing.

1	large mango, peeled and finely chopped
1	peach, peeled and finely chopped
1	orange or yellow bell pepper, seeded and finely chopped
1	cup finely chopped yellow tomato
½	cup chopped cilantro
¼	cup finely chopped red onion
2	teaspoons sugar
¼	teaspoon salt
	Juice of 1 lime

Mix together the mango, peach, bell pepper, tomato, cilantro, onion, sugar, salt, and lime juice in a medium-size bowl. Add more sugar, salt, and lime juice as desired. Makes 3 cups.

Surprise Flounder

THE SURPRISE nestled inside these lemon-dill fish foil packets is a pair of shrimp. For kids who don't like anything green (and perfumy), omit the dill.

INGREDIENTS:

4	tablespoons unsalted butter, at room temperature
1½	tablespoons minced shallot
2	garlic cloves, minced
1	teaspoon Dijon mustard
1	teaspoon salt
½	teaspoon pepper
4	flounder or sole filets
¼	cup lemon juice
4	thin slices of lemon
8	small shrimp
4	sprigs fresh dill

DIRECTIONS:

In a small bowl, mash together the butter, shallot, garlic, Dijon mustard, salt, and pepper with a fork.

Place 4 sheets of aluminum foil, each about 17 inches long, on your work surface. On each piece, center a fish filet, tucking in the ends so that the fish is an even thickness. Dot or spread the butter mixture over the filets. Sprinkle them with the lemon juice and top with a slice of lemon. Nestle 2 shrimp over each lemon slice and top with a sprig of dill.

Fold the foil into packets (for fun, you can make a fish shape by crimping one side of each packet into a C for a tail). Place the packets on a medium-hot grill or under an oven broiler for about 8 minutes, or until the fish is just cooked through. Serves 4.

KIDS' STEPS: Kids can mash together the butter mixture in a bowl and help wrap the fish in foil before grilling.

Prep time: 15 minutes Cooking time: 8 minutes

Fast Fish Fingers

KIDS AND PARENTS will devour these simple filet of sole fish sticks. The portions can also be jazzed up with the Homemade Tartar Sauce on page 53.

INGREDIENTS:

1 egg
1 tablespoon water
   Salt and pepper to taste
1 cup seasoned bread crumbs
2 tablespoons grated
   Parmesan cheese
2 **pounds filet of sole**
¼ **cup olive oil**
1 **lemon, cut into wedges**
   Tartar sauce (optional)

DIRECTIONS:
Crack open the egg into a bowl and add the water and salt and pepper to taste. Whisk well. In a separate bowl, mix the bread crumbs and Parmesan cheese. Rinse the fish and cut it into 4- by 2-inch sticks. Lightly coat the fish with the egg wash, then the bread crumbs.

Heat the olive oil in a large skillet over medium-high heat. Add the fish and cook until golden, about 3 minutes. Turn and repeat. Remove the fish from the pan and set on a dish lined with paper towels. Serve with lemon wedges and tartar sauce. Serves 6.

KIDS' STEPS: Kids can crack the egg and coat the fish with the egg wash and bread crumbs.

Prep time: 15 minutes   Cooking time: 8 minutes

Cooking Perfect Pasta

- One pound of dry pasta will feed about 5 people as a main course. The more extras you add to the dish — meats, beans, vegetables — the more it will feed.

- Once the water comes to a boil, add a tablespoon of olive oil to keep the noodles from sticking.

- Just before putting the pasta in the boiling water, add about 1 table-spoon of salt per 6 quarts of water (if you do it earlier, your pasta will taste bitter).

- Always bring the water to a rapid boil before adding pasta. Then cook the pasta uncovered, stirring occasionally. Otherwise, the noodles will become a big, rubbery wad.

- Cook pasta until it is just tender, checking a strand once a minute as it nears the end of its cooking time.

- Use a tablespoon of cold butter, cut into small pieces, as a predressing for hot pasta, no matter what sauce you're using.

World's Easiest Mac and Cheese

WHEN IT COMES to pleasing a child's palate, this savory classic is a pretty safe bet. Here's a super-simple version that is put together layer by layer, making it fun for kids to help prepare as well as eat.

INGREDIENTS:

- 1   pound elbow macaroni
      Butter (for greasing the dish)
- 3   cups milk
- 12 to 18 slices American cheese
- 12 Ritz crackers
      Salt
      Pepper
      Paprika

DIRECTIONS:

Cook and drain the elbow macaroni and let it cool slightly. Meanwhile, preheat the oven to 350° and grease a 13- by 9-inch baking pan or a large casserole dish.

Spoon a third of the pasta into the pan, then pour in 1 cup of the milk and cover it all with 4 to 6 slices of American cheese. Add two more layers of pasta, milk, and cheese in the same manner.

Next, crush a dozen Ritz crackers in a sealable plastic bag. Add salt and pepper and a dash of paprika, then sprinkle the crumbs over the top layer of pasta and cheese. Bake for 30 to 40 minutes or until bubbly. Serves 6 to 8.

KIDS' STEPS: Kids can help layer the cheese and pasta and crush the crackers for the topping.

Prep time: 15 minutes   Cooking time: 40 minutes

Pasta with Rainbow Veggies

THE SECRET to this dish is in cooking the ingredients together over low heat so the creamy sauce is absorbed into the noodles. To make a version that's not quite as rich, use light cream to replace up to half of the heavy cream.

INGREDIENTS:

- 2 tablespoons butter
- 1 or 2 garlic cloves, minced
- ½ cup chicken broth
- 1 pound asparagus, upper half of spears only, cut into 1-inch pieces
- 1 small zucchini or summer squash, cubed
- ½ cup finely diced carrot
- ½ cup diced red or yellow bell pepper
- 2 teaspoons salt for cooking the pasta, plus ¼ teaspoon for the sauce
- ¾ cup heavy cream
- 1 tablespoon olive oil
- ¾ pound fettuccine
- 1 cup freshly grated Parmesan cheese
- 2 tablespoons chopped fresh parsley

DIRECTIONS:

Heat 4 to 5 quarts of water to boiling.

Meanwhile, in an enameled Dutch oven or other large nonreactive casserole, melt the butter over low heat. Stir in the garlic and warm gently for 1 minute. Add the broth, vegetables, and ¼ teaspoon of salt. Bring the mixture to a simmer. Cover the pan and continue to simmer the vegetables undisturbed for 3 minutes. Then stir in the cream. Remove the pan from the heat and leave it covered. Add more salt to taste, if needed.

When the water comes to a boil, add the olive oil and the remainder of the salt. Bring to a boil again, then add the pasta. Cook according to the package directions, then drain. Bring the vegetables back to a simmer and add the drained pasta. Simmer the mixture over medium-low heat for 3 to 4 minutes while tossing the noodles up from the bottom of the pan with tongs or two forks. Remove the pan from the heat and sprinkle in half of the Parmesan cheese. Toss once more. Serve at once, using the parsley and remaining cheese for garnish. Serves 4 to 5.

KIDS' STEPS: Older kids can cut the asparagus, squash, and peppers.

Prep time: 30 minutes Cooking time: 15 minutes

Pasta with Pesto

Marinara Sauce

Many cooks simmer their marinara sauce all day to get the consistency and flavor just right — but this quick recipe only tastes as if it were prepared that way.

1   medium onion, finely chopped

3   tablespoons finely grated carrot (about $1/2$ small carrot)

$1^1/2$ tablespoons olive oil

2   garlic cloves, minced

1   28-ounce can crushed tomatoes

    Salt to taste

To make the tomato sauce, sauté the onion and carrot in the olive oil for 3 to 4 minutes over medium-high heat. Add the garlic and cook for another minute. Toss in the tomatoes and reduce the heat to medium, cooking another 10 to 15 minutes. Add salt to taste. Makes 3 cups of tomato sauce.

BRILLIANT GREEN and exploding with the flavors of summer, this variation on the classic pasta sauce has a secret ingredient: a sprig of parsley. Pesto means "pounded" in Italian, but we used a food processor for its speed and ease instead of the traditional mortar and pestle.

INGREDIENTS:

2   cups packed fresh basil leaves

4   sprigs Italian parsley

3   garlic cloves, crushed

1   teaspoon salt

$1/4$ cup pine nuts

$3/4$ cup olive oil
    Pepper to taste

$3/4$ cup grated Parmesan cheese

1   pound pasta, such as fusilli
    Cherry tomatoes, halved (optional)

DIRECTIONS:

In a food processor, combine the basil leaves, parsley, and garlic. Add the salt, pine nuts, and olive oil. Blend to a creamy butter consistency. Add more oil, if necessary, and pepper to taste. Finally, add the Parmesan cheese.

Cook the pasta according to the package directions. Drain it in a colander, then transfer to a large serving bowl. Toss with the pesto and garnish with cherry tomatoes, if desired. Serves 8 to 10.

TIP: If you are making pesto ahead of time, pour a thin layer of olive oil over the surface of the sauce to keep it fresh and green in the refrigerator. Pesto also freezes beautifully. To defrost, simply bring it to room temperature on a countertop (never heat it — heat dulls the bright color and flavor).

KIDS' STEPS: Kids can pull the basil leaves off their stems (a fun and fragrant job). Kids can also measure the ingredients and, with the help of an adult, whirl the pesto in the food processor.

Prep time: 15 minutes   Cooking time: 10 minutes

Spaghetti Pie

Cookbook author Molly Katzen proves that there are countless ways to give leftovers a new — and sometimes even better — life with her inspired dish made with day-old pasta.

INGREDIENTS:

	Olive oil
4	cups leftover spaghetti (or any cooked pasta)
1½	cups tomato sauce
10	fresh basil leaves, or 2 teaspoons dried (optional)
½	cup grated Parmesan cheese
¼	cup leftover vegetables such as olives, mushrooms, peppers (optional)
½	cup grated Monterey Jack or mozzarella cheese

DIRECTIONS:

Preheat the oven to 350°. Coat a 9-inch pie pan with a little olive oil (a pastry brush works well for this task), then set it aside. Place the spaghetti and the sauce in a large bowl and stir until the spaghetti is coated with the sauce. Working over the bowl, snip the basil with scissors or tear it by hand. Sprinkle in the Parmesan and stir well. If you want to get creative, toss in other leftovers from your fridge, such as olives or mushrooms — anything that seems appetizing.

Spread the spaghetti into the oiled pie pan and pat it down with the back of a wooden spoon. Sprinkle the Monterey Jack or mozzarella cheese on top and shake on a little extra Parmesan. Bake for 20 to 30 minutes, or until the pie turns brown and crispy on top. Cut into wedges and serve immediately with extra Parmesan cheese and tomato sauce. Serves 4.

KIDS' STEPS: Kids can stir the spaghetti together with the sauce (use a big bowl, so your child can enjoy mixing without fear of making a mess) and shake Parmesan cheese on top of the pie.

Prep time: 15 minutes   Cooking time: 30 minutes

Simple Spinach Lasagna

MAKING LASAGNA may seem like an ambitious project, but with this easy recipe, which calls for uncooked noodles and a trusted brand of tomato sauce, the process becomes accessible for even the youngest child (just in case you're looking for a helper).

INGREDIENTS:

- 2 pounds (4 cups) ricotta cheese
- 1 10-ounce package frozen spinach, defrosted and drained
- 5 garlic cloves, crushed
- 2 bunches fresh basil leaves
  Salt and pepper
- 1 28-ounce jar tomato sauce (or homemade)
- 10 uncooked lasagna noodles
- 1 pound mozzarella cheese, grated
  Grated Parmesan cheese

DIRECTIONS:

Place the ricotta cheese in a large bowl. Add the defrosted, well-drained spinach and garlic. Snip the basil leaves with scissors into the ricotta mixture. Add a little salt and pepper and stir until well blended.

Preheat the oven to 375°. Ladle 1 cup of the tomato sauce into a 13- by 9- by 2-inch baking pan. This recipe does not require precooking the lasagna noodles; the trick to making it work is adding this bottom layer of sauce, which provides extra moisture for the noodles to absorb.

Place a single layer of uncooked noodles on top of the sauce, then spoon half the ricotta mixture on top of the noodles, dropping it down in blobs here and there. You don't need to spread it unless you want to.

Pour half the remaining tomato sauce over the ricotta layer, then sprinkle with half the grated mozzarella. Add another layer of noodles, then more ricotta, then the remaining mozzarella.

Top with the rest of the sauce, cover tightly with foil, and bake for 40 minutes. Then remove the foil, sprinkle generously with grated Parmesan, and bake uncovered for another 30 minutes.

Remove the lasagna from the oven. Let it sit for about 15 minutes before slicing. Pass the Parmesan and—*mangia!* Serves 6 to 8.

KIDS' STEPS: Kids can mix up the ricotta cheese and spinach and help layer the lasagna.

PARTY IDEA
Kids' Cooking Party

Two things kids crave are food and fun. You can combine both these loves with a kids' lasagna cooking party.

Start by sending out invitations written on blank recipe cards. When the kids arrive, hand them paper chef hats and invite them to cook up their own lasagnas.

Give each child a disposable loaf pan (the type with plastic tops are best for sending home leftovers) and have them write their name in permanent marker on the side. Lay out all the lasagna ingredients in the middle of the table — precooked lasagna noodles, precooked meats (sausage and ground beef), tomato sauce, and cheeses (mozzarella, ricotta, Parmesan) — and let each child build a customized lasagna, starting with sauce at the bottom of the pan so the noodles won't stick.

Put the pans on a cookie sheet and bake at 300° for about 20 minutes or until the ingredients are warm and the cheeses have melted. Serve the lasagnas slightly cooled and let the kids eat right out of the pans.

Prep time: 25 minutes Cooking time: 70 minutes

Baked Ziti

THIS CHEESY RECIPE is popular with kids and quite easy to put together. Add a salad and Italian bread for a complete meal.

INGREDIENTS:

- ½ **pound box dried ziti**
- 16 **ounces ricotta cheese (part-skim)**
- 3 **cups shredded mozzarella cheese**
- 3 **cups spaghetti sauce**
- ½ **cup grated Parmesan cheese**

DIRECTIONS:
Preheat the oven to 350°. Bring a large pot of water to a boil and add the ziti. Cook until tender, about 8 minutes. Drain the pasta.

Place the ziti in a large bowl. Mix with the ricotta and half of the mozzarella. Grease a 9- by 13-inch casserole dish. Spread half of the spaghetti sauce on the bottom of the pan. Add the ziti mixture and cover with the remaining sauce. Sprinkle with Parmesan and the remaining mozzarella.

Bake for 20 to 30 minutes, or until the casserole bubbles on the edges. Serves 6.

KIDS' STEPS: Kids can mix the ziti and cheeses and spread the spaghetti sauce in the casserole dish.

Prep time: 25 minutes Cooking time: 30 minutes

American Chop Suey

THIS DINNERTIME FAVORITE goes by a few aliases. Some call it American chop suey; others, goulash, after a Hungarian dish of meat and vegetables. Whatever your family calls it, this simple pasta recipe is also the perfect first endeavor for a budding young chef.

INGREDIENTS:
- 1 **pound box elbow macaroni**
- 1 **medium onion, chopped**
  Olive or vegetable oil
- 1 **pound lean ground beef**
  Salt and pepper
- 1 **28-ounce jar pasta sauce**
- ¼ **cup, plus garnish, grated Parmesan cheese**

DIRECTIONS:
Cook the pasta according to the package directions. Drain in a colander.

Sauté the onion in a little oil, then add the meat and cook over medium-high heat until done. Drain the grease from the pan, then add salt and pepper to taste.

In a large saucepan (you can use the one you cooked the pasta in), combine the sauce, the ¼ cup Parmesan cheese, and the beef mixture and bring to a simmer. Add the cooked pasta, turn off the heat, and let it sit for 5 to 10 minutes before serving. Garnish individual portions with the additional grated cheese. Serves 8.

KIDS' STEPS: Older kids can help sauté the onions and brown the ground beef.

BREADS WE LOVE
Garlic Bread Galore

For restaurant-quality garlic bread, follow these easy recipes.

GARLIC BUTTER

Using a food processor or electric mixer, blend 4 tablespoons of room temperature butter or margarine with 1 to 2 crushed garlic cloves. For melted garlic butter, microwave the butter, then add the crushed garlic cloves. Mix in fresh basil or parsley to give the butter extra color and flavor.

NOTHING FANCY GARLIC BREAD

Cut a loaf of French bread into 1-inch slices (but not all the way through the bottom crust) and spread each slice with garlic butter. Wrap in foil and bake in a preheated 350° oven for 5 minutes or until heated through.

CRISPY GARLIC BREAD

Brush both sides of 1-inch rounds of French bread with melted garlic butter. Place on a cookie sheet and broil each side until golden.

GARLIC STICKS

Cut a loaf of French bread the long way and spread with garlic butter or brush with melted garlic butter. Broil, cut side up, until brown. Cut into 1-inch slices.

Prep time: 15 minutes   Cooking time: 20 minutes

Peanut Butter Noodles

MY GREAT IDEA
Leftover Café

"We always seem to have small portions of several different leftovers that no one wants to eat, so I devised a way to use them up. I used the computer to design a menu that listed all the leftovers and put one menu at each place at the dinner table. My ten-year-old son, Will, saw the menu and said, 'Wow! There are so many great choices!'— a much better reaction than I received when I used the word 'leftovers.' If everyone tries to order the same thing, I tell them the kitchen has only one or two orders left. The 'tasting platter' option, a little bit of everything, is the most popular dish."

— Kimberly Kroener
Larkspur, California

T HIS NUTTY NOODLE dish is everything a kid could want: sweet, salty, crunchy, and slathered in peanut butter. The thin noodles cook quickly and are served cold, making this a perfect light supper.

INGREDIENTS:

1   pound linguini, angel hair pasta, or soba noodles
½   cup creamy peanut butter
5   tablespoons rice wine vinegar
5   tablespoons sesame oil
4   tablespoons soy sauce
2   teaspoons peeled and grated fresh ginger root
1   small garlic clove, crushed

OPTIONAL TOPPINGS:

Grated carrot, scallion (sliced into rounds), cucumber (peeled, seeded, and thinly sliced), toasted sesame seeds, and chopped peanuts
4   scallions, trimmed and cut

DIRECTIONS:

Cook the noodles according to the package directions, then drain and rinse with cold water. In a large bowl, blend together the peanut butter, vinegar, sesame oil, soy sauce, ginger, and garlic. Add the noodles or pasta, toss well, then garnish with the toppings. Serve at room temperature. Serves 4 to 6.

KIDS' STEPS: Kids can measure and mix ingredients and crush garlic in the garlic press.

Prep time: 15 minutes Cooking time: 5 minutes

Perfect Pizza

PIZZA IS SURPRISINGLY quick to make — it takes about as long as it does to get one delivered. What's more, kids are enthralled with the process — kneading and shaping the dough, then designing pies with favorite toppings. To make a pie even more quickly, use store-bought pizza dough from your grocery store.

INGREDIENTS:

DOUGH:

- ½ cup warm water
- 1 teaspoon active dry yeast
- ¼ teaspoon salt
- 1 tablespoon olive oil, plus extra for coating
- 1¼ cups all-purpose flour, plus extra for dusting

TOPPINGS:

- Sliced mushrooms, green peppers, broccoli, olives, or pepperoni
- 1 cup tomato sauce
- 1½ cups grated mozzarella cheese
- 1½ cups grated Muenster cheese

DIRECTIONS:

To make the dough, place the warm water in a large bowl and sprinkle on the yeast. Let stand for 5 minutes, or until foamy.

Add the salt, oil, and ½ cup flour and beat the mixture with a wooden spoon for a minute or two. Add the remaining flour and keep mixing.

When the dough gets too stiff for the spoon, mix with clean hands. Add a bit of extra flour, if necessary, to make a soft, smooth dough. Knead on a floured board for 5 minutes. Transfer to a lightly oiled bowl, cover, and let rise for about 30 minutes.

Heat the oven to 450°. Punch down the risen dough, turn it out onto a floured board, and knead for a few minutes.

Divide into two equal parts and roll each portion into a large round. Place each on a lightly oiled baking sheet. If you are using a preheated pizza stone, sprinkle some cornmeal onto a pizza peel (a wooden paddle) and place the dough on the peel.

Spread a thin layer of sauce on the crust — not too much, or else your pizza will become soggy.

Top your pizzas with the mozzarella and Muenster cheeses and garnish with the toppings of your choice. Bake for 12 to 15 minutes; subtract a few minutes if you're using a pizza stone. When done, the crusts will be golden underneath. Makes 2 medium-size pizzas.

FUN FOOD
Pizza Fish

To make the pepperoni pizza fish pictured above, first heat the oven to 450°. For each fish, roll a portion of pizza dough into an oval and place it on a baking sheet. Pinch in the dough to create a tail.

Spread sauce on the "fish," leaving a ½-inch border and top with cheese. Start an inch or two in from the face of the fish and vertically overlap pepperoni slices to make scales. Add an olive eye on the face, as shown. Bake 15 minutes, or until the underside of the crust is golden brown.

KIDS' STEPS: Kids can help mix and knead the pizza dough, prepare toppings, and assemble the pizzas.

**Prep time: 15 minutes Rising time: 30 minutes
Cooking time: 15 minutes**

CHAPTER THREE

Side Dishes

I F THERE'S ONE lesson that Thanksgiving teaches us besides gratitude, of course, it's that side dishes make the meal. When you pass around the creamy mashed potatoes, fresh baby peas, and sweet potato pie, just watch the clamoring begin.

In this chapter you'll find recipes for comforting favorites — Cheese-stuffed Baked Potatoes (page 76) and Candy Carrot Coins (page 73) — plus a few wholesome takes on fast-food-style faves, such as Onion Rings (page 72) and Oven-baked French Fries (page 79). Whether tried-and-true or new contenders, what these recipes have in common are speed, simplicity, and great kid appeal.

Keep it simple. Even a quick recipe is hardly a time-saver if it dirties every dish in the house. Many of the dishes here, such as Smoky Rice and Beans (page 75) and Chinese Fried Rice (page 74), boast one-pot preparation, and do double duty, combining a starch and a vegetable. Streamline dinner preparation whenever you can (why not throw some potatoes into the oven with that roasting chicken?) and feel free to adapt recipes to use the ingredients you have on hand.

Serve veggies first. There's no need to approach "side dishes" too literally. If your kids snack on a dish of red pepper strips while you make dinner, pat yourself on the back for a vegetable successfully prepared and eaten. If they nibble peas and cherry tomatoes in the garden, count that as a serving. Remember, too, that kids often prefer the taste of raw vegetables to cooked ones.

Eat the rainbow. When it comes to food, variety — of color, texture, and flavor — is truly the spice of life. Eating a selection of vegetables and other side dishes greatly increases the chances of you and your family getting all the nutrients you need for good health. Over the course of a week, encourage your family to eat all of the colors in the rainbow: green (beans, peas, zucchini), orange (sweet potatoes, winter squash, and carrots), and red (tomatoes, beets, and red cabbage).

Offer fruit as a side dish. If your kids refuse to eat spinach or peas, serve them apples, pears, or strawberries. Although they taste sweeter, fruits are often just as nutritious as vegetables.

Expand their horizons. Side dishes make perfect testing grounds for new tastes. Since they're not the main components of a meal, side dishes allow you to risk serving a food your child might not eat. And you just might be surprised at how much he likes it! A bit of sesame oil and ginger may open the door to Chinese food; a sprinkle of cumin may welcome your child into the world of spice; and one unusual food, like yam chips (page 78), just might give him the confidence to sample others.

Cheese-stuffed Baked Potatoes, page 76

Pick a Veggie, Any Veggie

"When my son, Tony, was a pre-schooler, he wanted to help with the grocery shopping. He picked item after item off every shelf. After replacing each item, I finally hit upon a place in the store where Tony could choose whatever he wanted — the produce aisle. Eating has been an adventure ever since.

"The first thing Tony wanted to try was brussels sprouts. He didn't know he was supposed to hate them, and I didn't fill him in. That night at dinner, he eagerly bit into a steamed sprout and declared, 'It's great!'

"Over the past two years, we've tried eggplant, asparagus, and caram-bola. And the discoveries have spread beyond the produce aisle. Tony has selected a variety of fish and unusual meats like buffalo. I've discovered flavors from different lands and have even fought with my son over the last serving of squash. He's quit turning up his nose at new foods, and now he's the one in the family who says, 'Just taste it.'"

— *Amy Nappa*
Loveland, Colorado

Sugar Snap Peas and Yogurt Dip

SUGAR SNAPS are delicious alone, but when served with this dip, the peas are even more enticing.

INGREDIENTS:

   1 pound sugar snap peas
   ⅔ cup plain yogurt
   ¼ cup honey
   2 teaspoons Dijon mustard

DIRECTIONS:

Pinch the flower ends off the peas and remove the strings. Bring a large saucepan of lightly salted water to a rapid boil. Add the sugar snaps. Immediately drain them in a colander, then plunge the peas into a bowl of ice water for 5 minutes. Drain and pat them dry.

For the dip, combine the yogurt, honey, and mustard in a bowl. Place snap peas around the dip. Serves 6.

KIDS' STEPS: Kids can measure and stir the dip for the peas.

Prep time: 5 minutes Cooking time: 10 minutes

Mud and Trees

INVITE YOUR KIDS to dip fresh broccoli florets (trees) into this tasty peanut dip (mud).

INGREDIENTS:

       Broccoli florets
   1 cup smooth peanut butter
   ¼ cup cider vinegar
   3 tablespoons soy sauce
   1 tablespoon brown sugar
   ¾ to 1 cup water
       Up to 1 teaspoon cayenne
          pepper or hot sauce

DIRECTIONS:

For emerald-green broccoli florets, drop them into a large pot of boiling water for 1 minute, drain, then plunge them into a large bowl of ice water until cool.

In a blender, combine the peanut butter, cider vinegar, soy sauce, and brown sugar. Add the water and blend, stopping and mixing with a spoon once or twice to combine (peanut butters vary in texture, so add just enough water to make the mixture dip consistency). Finally, spice it up with as little or as much cayenne pepper or hot sauce as you like. Makes about 2 cups sauce.

KIDS' STEPS: Kids can press the buttons on the blender to mix up the dip.

Prep time: 10 minutes Cooking time: 5 minutes

Homemade Onion Rings

FAT-FREE, HERB-SEASONED crouton crumbs add texture and flavor to these onion rings without adding hassle — or fat. In fact, a serving of these rings contains 75 percent less fat and 60 percent fewer calories than a fast-food equivalent. Don't be put off by the nonalcoholic beer: its bubbles help leaven the batter, and its flavor blends right in.

INGREDIENTS:

- 3 medium (or 2 large) yellow or sweet onions
- 1 cup all-purpose flour
- 1 cup nonalcoholic beer
- ¼ teaspoon cayenne pepper (optional)
- ½ teaspoon seasoning salt
- ¼ teaspoon pepper
- 2 egg whites, beaten to soft peaks
- 1 5-ounce bag fat-free herb-flavored croutons (crushed or processed into 2 cups of fine crumbs)
- 2 tablespoons canola oil Canola cooking spray (see left)

DIRECTIONS:

Heat the oven to 450°. Cut the onions into ½-inch-thick slices and separate them into rings; reserve the smallest inner rings for another recipe. In a large, deep bowl, combine the flour, beer, cayenne pepper (if desired), seasoning salt, and pepper and whisk together. Gently fold in the egg whites; the batter should be light and fluffy.

Spread the crouton crumbs in a shallow bowl. Coat 2 baking sheets with 1 tablespoon of canola oil each. Hook an onion ring on your finger and dip it into the batter, shaking off excess. Then dip it into the crouton crumbs and shake off the excess. Place the ring on one of the prepared sheets. Repeat with the remaining onions and batter, placing the smaller rings inside the large ones to make use of every inch of the pan. Spray the tops generously with canola cooking spray. Bake for 18 to 20 minutes, flipping after 10 minutes, until lightly browned. Makes 8 servings.

KIDS' STEPS: Kids can whisk eggs, dip the onion rings into the batter and crouton crumbs, and shake off the excess.

Prep time: 25 minutes   Baking time: 20 minutes

Candy Carrot Coins

Tossed with a glaze of brown sugar and butter, these carrots taste slightly sweet and look perfectly shiny.

INGREDIENTS:
- 1 pound carrots
- 1 tablespoon butter
- 2 tablespoons brown sugar
- 1 teaspoon water

DIRECTIONS:
Peel the carrots, then slice each one into rounds. Place the carrot coins in a microwave-safe bowl, cover them with water, and cover the bowl with plastic wrap. Microwave for 6 to 7 minutes, or until the carrots are tender but not mushy. Drain the water and set the carrots aside.

In a small frying pan, melt the butter, stir in the brown sugar and water, and cook for 1 minute. Add the carrot coins and toss to coat with the brown-sugar mixture. Cook on low for 3 to 4 minutes, or until the carrots are thoroughly glazed. Makes 4 servings.

KIDS' STEPS: Older kids can peel and slice the carrots, use the microwave, and make the glaze.

FUN FOOD
Carrot Curls

No, it's not the latest hairstyle or a weight-lifting challenge — it's a clever yet simple presentation to lure kids who normally turn up their noses at this root vegetable. Just use a vegetable peeler to slice a carrot into long strips. Eat as is or roll each piece and spear it with a toothpick. For even more drama and flavor, dunk the curls in Silly-dilly Dip (below).

SILLY-DILLY DIP

Mix $1/2$ cup low-fat sour cream, $1/2$ teaspoon dried dill, $1/4$ teaspoon garlic powder, $1/4$ teaspoon onion powder, and 1 pinch salt in a bowl. Makes $1/2$ cup dip.

Prep time: 10 minutes Cooking time: 12 minutes

Using Chopsticks

Chinese food just seems to taste better when you eat it with chopsticks. Using them is also a great way to slow the meal to an enjoyable pace. Granted, handling chopsticks can be a bit tricky at first, but with a little practice, your child will be able to wield them like a pro. Just cradle one chopstick in the curve between your thumb and index finger so that it rests on the tip of your ring finger. Set the second stick above the first, grasping it as you would a pencil. Now hold the bottom stick steady and move the top stick up and down. In time, you should be able to pick up even a single grain of rice.

Chinese Fried Rice

IF YOU HAVE leftover rice from last night's dinner, turn it into tonight's side dish with this easy recipe. Make sure to use cold rice instead of warm rice, so that the finished dish is not mushy. Add cooked beef or chicken to this stir-fry to make it a complete meal.

INGREDIENTS:

2½ tablespoons vegetable oil
½ teaspoon sesame oil
4 scallions, sliced
1 cup frozen baby peas, thawed
1 medium carrot, peeled and grated
3 cups cooked and chilled long-grain white rice
3 large eggs
1½ to 2 tablespoons soy sauce

DIRECTIONS:

Heat 2 tablespoons of the vegetable oil and all of the sesame oil in a large sauté pan or wok over medium heat. Add the scallions, peas, and grated carrot all at once, taking care to avoid being splattered by hot oil. Sauté the vegetables for 1 minute, stirring them constantly. Add the rice and heat for 2 to 3 minutes, stirring occasionally.

Break the eggs into a small bowl and beat them with a fork or small whisk until blended. Then push the rice to the perimeter of the pan and pour the remaining ½ tablespoon of vegetable oil into the center. Add the eggs and stir them continuously with a wooden spoon until they are soft but not overcooked.

When the eggs are almost fully cooked, stir the rice in until everything is well mixed. Add the soy sauce and heat for another minute or two, stirring often. Makes 4 servings.

KIDS' STEPS: Kids can measure the rice and peas and whisk the eggs (older kids can also scramble the eggs in the pan).

Prep time: 10 minutes Cooking time: 10 minutes

Smoky Rice and Beans

THE SECRET INGREDIENT in this rice dish is chipotle peppers (smoked jalapeños, available in cans at your supermarket). Just a touch of these peppers gives this dish a slightly smoky flavor, which makes it a great complement to the Chicken Fajitas on page 41.

INGREDIENTS:

1 tablespoon olive oil
½ cup diced onion
½ teaspoon ground cumin
1 teaspoon minced canned
     chipotle pepper

1 cup white rice
1 cup canned black beans,
     drained and rinsed
½ cup canned diced
     tomatoes, drained
½ cup frozen corn (optional)
   Salt and pepper
2 cups chicken broth
2 tablespoons chopped
     scallion greens
     (optional)

DIRECTIONS:

Heat the olive oil in a medium-size saucepan over medium heat. Add the onion, cumin, and chipotle pepper. Cook for 5 minutes, stirring occasionally, until the onion starts to soften.

Add the rice and stir to coat with the oil. Add the black beans, tomatoes, and corn, if desired. Season with salt and pepper. Pour in the chicken broth and bring to a boil. Reduce the heat to low, cover, and simmer for about 25 minutes, or until all the liquid is absorbed.

Remove from the heat and let stand for 10 minutes. Transfer to a serving bowl, then sprinkle with scallions, if desired. Makes 4 to 6 servings.

KIDS' STEPS: Kids can rinse and drain the canned beans and tomatoes and measure the rice and frozen corn.

Prep time: 15 minutes   Cooking time: 40 minutes

Cheese-stuffed Baked Potatoes

THESE MASHED POTATOES, packed inside a crunchy skin, can be baked along with the Roast Chicken on page 38. Four potatoes should be enough for six to eight people, since you're cutting the potatoes in half and the filling is rich.

INGREDIENTS:

- 4 medium freshly baked potatoes
- 1 cup grated extra-sharp Cheddar cheese
- ¼ cup grated Parmesan cheese
- ½ cup sour cream (for a lower-fat dish, use ½ cup plain yogurt or ⅓ cup milk)
- 2 to 4 tablespoons unsalted butter
- ½ cup minced onion
- 2 garlic cloves, crushed
  Salt to taste

DIRECTIONS:

Split the freshly baked potatoes in half while they're still hot. Carefully scrape the insides into a large bowl, saving the skins. Add the cheeses, sour cream, butter, onion, and garlic. Mash well and add salt to taste.

Stuff this mixture back into the potato skins. Return the potatoes to the oven and bake at 400° until the tops are golden brown. Serves 6 to 8.

VEGGIE TWICE-BAKED POTATOES
For this variation, chop 1 small bag of frozen mixed vegetables (thawed) in a food processor and add along with the cheeses and sour cream before mashing.

KIDS' STEPS: Kids can scrub and poke the potatoes with a fork, then help mash them after they are cooked.

Prep time: 10 minutes   Baking time: 10 minutes

Mashed Potato Clouds

ACCORDING TO OUR kid testers, smashing and mushing the cooked potatoes with an old-fashioned potato masher is the best part of making this classic side dish.

INGREDIENTS:

6 medium-size russet or Idaho potatoes
2 teaspoons salt (for cooking)
¼ to ½ cup milk
4 tablespoons butter
½ cup sour cream
Salt and pepper to taste

DIRECTIONS:

Peel the potatoes and cut out any brown spots. Cut each potato in half lengthwise and then slice into ½- to 1-inch pieces. You should have about 6 cups of peeled potatoes.

Place the potatoes in a saucepan and cover with cold water by a cou-ple of inches. Add about 2 teaspoons of salt to the water.

Bring the potatoes to a boil over medium-high heat, watching carefully to make sure they do not boil over. Once they have come to a boil, cook for an additional 10 minutes or until tender (about 20 minutes in all). Take the pan of potatoes off the stove and drain the water.

Pour the milk and scatter slices of the butter over the potatoes. Spoon the sour cream here and there over the hot potatoes as well. Wait several minutes for the butter to melt and the sour cream to warm. **NOTE:** If you are working with younger kids, transfer the potatoes from the hot saucepan to a large bowl before mashing.

With a potato masher, press down repeatedly on the potatoes until they are smooth. Makes 6 servings.

KIDS' STEPS: Older kids can peel the potatoes. Kids as young as three can help mash them.

TIP: When mashing potatoes, lift the masher up, then press down until the potatoes are smooth and relatively lump-free. Don't mash for more than a few minutes, or the potatoes will develop a gluelike consistency (don't use a food processor for the same reason).

FUN FOOD
Volcano Potatoes

With its flowing layer of bubbling, cheesy lava, this active 'tater crater takes ordinary mashed potatoes to new heights.

First, mash four cooked russet potatoes, adding butter, milk, salt, and pepper to taste. To make the cheese topping, whip ¼ cup whipping cream with an electric beater until it's stiff, then fold in ½ cup shredded American or Cheddar cheese.

Heat the oven to 350°. Cover a cookie sheet with aluminum foil, then coat with cooking spray. Spoon prepared mashed potatoes onto the sheet and shape into a mountainous pile.

Use a spoon to carve out a hole ½ inch deep at the top of the volcano and fill it with the cheese mixture. (You can also use a fork to add cracks and crevices to the sides of your mountain.) Bake the volcano for 20 minutes, or until the cheese is hot and bubbly. Makes 6 to 8 servings.

Prep time: 10 minutes   Cooking time: 20 minutes

Yam Chips

For a quick and healthy side dish, cook up a batch of oven-baked yam chips. Heat the oven to 425°. Cut 1 pound of yams or sweet potatoes (3 small or 2 medium) into thin slices, about ⅛ inch thick. Put the slices into a large sealable plastic bag. Add 1½ tablespoons olive oil, ½ teaspoon salt, and 2 teaspoons herb blend. (We used Frontier all-purpose salt-free seasoning. Italian herb blends or Mrs. Dash would also work.) Seal the bag and shake to coat.

Line a cookie sheet with aluminum foil and coat the foil with cooking spray. Place the yam slices on the sheet and bake for 25 minutes, or until the chips are golden brown, flipping once during cooking time. Makes 4 servings.

Sweet-potato Pie

YOUR KIDS MAY crinkle their noses at the idea of eating sweet potatoes, but this version, with toasty marshmallows, is sure to stick with them.

INGREDIENTS:

- 3 large sweet potatoes, cooked until tender, or one 29-ounce can of sweet potatoes
- 1 egg
- ⅓ cup sugar
- ½ teaspoon cinnamon
- 1 teaspoon vanilla extract
- 2 cups mini marshmallows

DIRECTIONS:
Heat the oven to 350°. Combine the sweet potatoes, egg, sugar, cinnamon, and vanilla extract in a bowl and mix with an electric mixer on medium speed for 2 to 3 minutes. Empty the mixture into a 2-quart ungreased baking dish. Bake uncovered for 25 minutes. Top with the marshmallows and bake for an additional 5 minutes. Serves 4 to 6.

NOTE: This dish can be frozen, but don't add the marshmallows or bake it before freezing.

KIDS' STEPS: Kids can arrange the marshmallows on top of the sweet potatoes to look like fluffy clouds.

Prep time: 10 minutes Baking time: 30 minutes

Oven-baked French Fries

CRAVING FRENCH FRIES but want something with a little more flair? These seasoned, battered, and oven-baked potato wedges taste darn close to the restaurant version but contain 70 percent less fat and 40 percent fewer calories.

INGREDIENTS:

2 tablespoons canola oil
1 cup all-purpose flour
1 teaspoon garlic powder
1 teaspoon salt
1 teaspoon black pepper
½ teaspoon celery salt
½ teaspoon seasoning salt
2 large eggs
4 medium potatoes, scrubbed and rinsed but not peeled
   Canola cooking spray (see page 72)

DIRECTIONS:

Heat the oven to 450°. Coat a baking sheet with a tablespoon of canola oil. With a fork or whisk, mix the flour, garlic powder, salt, pepper, celery salt, and seasoning salt in a shallow dish and set aside. Beat the eggs in a small bowl.

Cut the potatoes into wedges ½-inch thick. Dip each wedge into the beaten eggs, then into the flour mixture, making sure it is well coated. Place the wedges on the prepared baking sheet and let them sit 10 to 15 minutes. Coat the tops of the potato wedges generously with canola cooking spray. Bake in the center of the oven until golden brown, 15 to 18 minutes, flipping after 10 minutes. Makes 5 servings.

KIDS' STEPS: Kids can mix up the coating for the french fries, crack and whisk the eggs, and dip the potato wedges into the egg wash and coating.

FUN FOOD
Potato Turkeys

If your kids are wandering around the kitchen antsy for dinner, let them dress up a crowd of potato turkeys for a zany table decoration.

Begin with a plain potato and stand it up with a toothpick tripod (later, the kids can use peanut butter to attach pretzel stick feet over the toothpicks to conceal them). Put out an assortment of fresh and dried fruits, nuts, vegetables, and pretzels. Let each child use toothpicks to attach soft items to the potato body. Attach hard items, like nuts and raisins, with peanut butter.

Prep time: 30 minutes   Baking time: 18 minutes

CHAPTER FOUR

What's for Dessert?

Now, FOR THE fun part. Dessert is the icing on the cake, so to speak. And on a weeknight when everybody is feeling tired and frazzled, it can be extra-nice to have a trick or two up your sleeve.

Take our Fresh Fruit and Chocolate Sauce (page 84), for example: all that stands between it and a piece of fresh fruit is a handful of chocolate chips melted with a little cream. But watch your kids light up as they skewer strawberries for dipping, and you'll feel like you've put on a magic show.

That's our aim here: lots of "wow" without a lot of fiddling or fancy ingredients. Many of these recipes can bake or chill in the time that dinner takes to cook and eat, and those few minutes of preparation will feel worthwhile. Hand out slices of Brownie Pizza (page 89) or some Raspberry Cream Pops (page 83), and even the simplest family meal will feel like a party.

Take shortcuts. Many of our recipes require only a little doctoring of store-bought ingredients. Ice cream and cookies, for instance, become Easy Ice-cream Sandwiches (page 85). Feel free to further simplify recipes, as your schedule dictates. And when all else fails, remember that a plate of attractively sliced fruit or packaged cookies makes a perfectly acceptable finale.

Strategize sweetly. Many of our desserts keep well, especially the cookies, bars, and frozen treats, so they make great candidates for make-ahead meal enders. Spend an hour on the weekend or after school baking or concocting with your kids, and the results will be sweet indeed.

Hire your child as a pastry chef. Dessert-making is the perfect occasion to give your child some autonomy in the kitchen. Supervise any steps that require stove time or cutting, but let your child do the rest. Think how proud she'll feel when she pulls a brownie from her lunch box the next day and knows she made it herself.

Keep butter, flour, and sugar on hand for dessert-making. You'll be more inclined to bake from scratch if you keep baking essentials in your kitchen cupboards. For best results, just be sure to measure the ingredients in a recipe precisely. Unlike cooking, baking is a science and you need to follow the recipe to a T.

Avoid offering a sweet reward. Nutritionists discourage using sugary desserts as a reward for good behavior or good eating. But every family has its own solution to the dessert dilemma. On days when you feel your kids have not been eating as well as they should, offer up fresh fruit for a healthy dessert.

Banana Cream Pie, page 93

Raspberry Cream Pops

T O M A K E this cool and healthy treat, we combined the delicate sweetness of raspberries with the creaminess of vanilla yogurt. The pops take several hours to freeze, so prepare them in the morning if you're planning on serving them after dinner.

INGREDIENTS:
- 1   pint raspberries
- ½   cup sugar
- 1¼ cups water
- ½   cup cream (heavy or light)
- 1   tablespoon lemon juice
- 1   cup vanilla yogurt
- 8   5-ounce waxy paper cups
- 8   Popsicle sticks

DIRECTIONS:
In a blender, puree ¾ of the pint of raspberries with the sugar and water. Then use a jelly bag or sieve to strain out the seeds (this should yield about 2 cups of pulp).

Transfer ⅔ cup of the raspberry puree into a separate container, add the cream, and whisk well to mix. Meanwhile, stir the lemon juice into the rest of the raspberry puree. Now, you should have two containers of raspberry sauce — one that's deep red and another that's creamy pink. Chill both sauces.

In a bowl, stir together the vanilla yogurt and the remaining raspberries. Pour the mixture into the paper cups until they are about half full. Set the cups in an 8- by 8-inch pan (for transferring them easily in and out of the freezer). Cover each cup with aluminum foil and poke a Popsicle stick straight through the center of the foil and into the mixture. Freeze until set (about 2 hours).

Remove the foil and pour a layer of the deep red puree on top of the frozen yogurt. Freeze again until solid (about 2 hours). Finally, pour a layer of the raspberry cream mixture into each cup and freeze until solid. To serve, peel the cups away from the pops. Makes 8 pops.

KIDS' STEPS: Kids can measure the ingredients and stir them together, push the buttons on the blender, and stir the yogurt into the raspberry puree.

Fresh Fruit and Chocolate Sauce

QUICK HIT

Dipped Strawberries

In a hurry to put dessert on the table? Here's a delicious treat that requires no baking at all. First, wash and pat dry a pint of strawberries. In a small bowl, beat together 8 ounces of cream cheese and 3 tablespoons of milk and put the mixture in a bowl on the table along with the berries and a container of brown sugar. When you're ready to eat, dip the berries first in the cream, then in the sugar.

THIS SWEET DESSERT is quick and easy to assemble, and kids and grownups alike will enjoy skewering their own selection of fruits and dipping them into the melted chocolate.

INGREDIENTS:
CHOCOLATE SAUCE:

- 12 ounces semisweet chocolate chips
- ⅔ cup heavy cream

FRUIT DIPPERS:

- 1 pint fresh strawberries, washed and hulled
- 1 cup fresh pineapple chunks
- 2 bananas, cut into chunks
- 2 cups cubed store-bought angel food cake

DIRECTIONS:
CHOCOLATE SAUCE:

In a medium saucepan, heat the chocolate chips and cream over low heat, stirring often, until the chips have melted. Transfer the chocolate to a warm fondue pot (or keep it on the stove on low) to keep it warm for dipping.

FRUIT DIPPERS:

Spear fresh strawberries, pineapple, bananas, and cake with fondue forks or skewers and dip them into the warm chocolate sauce. Serves 6 to 8.

KIDS' STEPS: With supervision, kids can help stir the melting chocolate chips and cream, then dip the fruits into the warm chocolate sauce.

Prep time: 15 minutes Cooking time: 5 minutes

Easy Ice-cream Sandwiches

YOU WON'T GET the cold shoulder when you serve these sandwiches for dessert tonight. You can make them with almost any of your favorite cookies (homemade or store-bought) and ice-cream flavors. Here are a few kid-friendly combinations.

INGREDIENTS:
- Store-bought cookies or chocolate graham crackers
- Ice cream
- Chopped nuts, optional

DIRECTIONS:

PEANUT BUTTER CHOCOLATE
Top a peanut butter cookie (set face-down) with a scoop of slightly softened chocolate ice cream. Set a second cookie right side up on the ice cream and gently press down. Now roll the sandwich on edge in chopped peanuts (it takes about 2 tablespoons per 3-inch sandwich). Wrap in aluminum foil and freeze until ready to eat.

OATMEAL PECAN
Spread softened butter pecan ice cream (maple walnut works well, too) between oatmeal cookies.

VANILLA FUDGE
Sandwich slabs of vanilla fudge swirl ice cream between chocolate graham crackers. Wrap and freeze for at least 1 day so the crackers will soften.

KIDS' STEPS: Kids can place the top cookie over the ice cream and roll the sandwich in the chopped nuts.

Prep time: 15 minutes   Freezing time: up to 24 hours

Forget endlessly cranking the handle of an ice-cream maker. After combining the following ingredients, each family member can simply shake up his or her own pouch of soft serve — and it's done in just 5 minutes.

NOTE: The bigger the salt granules, the better. Kosher or rock salt works best, but table salt is fine.

2   tablespoons of sugar

1   cup half-and-half

1/2 teaspoon vanilla extract

1/2 cup salt

     Ice cubes (enough to fill a
         gallon-size bag about half full)

Combine the sugar, half-and-half, and vanilla extract in a pint-size sealable bag and seal tightly. Place the salt and ice in the gallon-size bag, then place the sealed smaller bag inside as well. Seal the larger bag. Now shake the bags about 5 minutes, until the mixture hardens. Feel the small bag to determine when it's done. Take the smaller bag out of the larger one and add mix-ins. Serve the ice cream in a bowl or, for fun, eat it right out of the bag. Easy cleanup, too! Serves 1.

DON'T BE DECEIVED by the photograph. Even though this dessert looks elegant, it's a cinch to make. Our kid testers enjoyed swirling the purple sauce through the cream.

INGREDIENTS:

1   tablespoon butter

2   cups blueberries, stemmed
         and rinsed

1/3 cup sugar

1½   cups cold heavy cream

DIRECTIONS:

In a saucepan, melt the butter over medium heat and then stir in the blueberries and sugar. Cover and cook, stirring occasionally, about 10 minutes, until the blueberries release their juices. Let cool.

Puree the berries in a blender or food processor. Refrigerate the sauce until completely cooled. Pour the heavy cream into a large, chilled mixing bowl and beat it with an electric mixer until soft peaks form. Reserve ¼ cup of the blueberry sauce, then use a spatula to fold the remaining sauce into the whipped cream until thoroughly combined.

Spoon the Blueberry Fool into 6 ramekins or small parfait glasses. Spoon some of the reserved blueberry sauce around the edges of each serving, then use a knife to swirl the sauce throughout the dessert. Refrigerate until you are ready to eat. Serves 6.

KIDS' STEPS: Older kids can stir the blueberry sauce while it heats and use a knife to swirl the sauce through the dessert after it cools.

Prep time: 10 minutes Cooking time: 10 minutes

Butterscotch Pudding

OLD-FASHIONED cornstarch puddings like this one are perennial crowd pleasers and deserve to be in every family's recipe file.

INGREDIENTS:

- 2 tablespoons sugar
- ¼ cup cornstarch
- 3 cups half-and-half or milk
- 3 large egg yolks
   Pinch of salt
- 4 tablespoons unsalted butter
- ½ cup packed dark brown sugar
- ½ teaspoon vanilla extract

DIRECTIONS:

In a medium mixing bowl, stir the sugar and cornstarch until blended. Be sure to break up any clumps of cornstarch to ensure that the finished pudding will be smooth. Add 1½ cups of the half-and-half or milk, the egg yolks, and the salt, then whisk until everything is well blended. Set aside.

Melt the butter in a medium saucepan over moderate heat. Add the brown sugar to the pan. Continue heating the mixture, stirring constantly, until it begins to bubble.

Gradually whisk the remaining 1½ cups of half-and-half or milk into the pan. When the liquid is hot (not boiling) and the brown sugar has dissolved, remove it from the heat. Using a ladle, add the hot liquid to the reserved liquid in the mixing bowl one scoop at a time, gently whisking all the while.

Pour all of the liquid back into the saucepan and cook over moderate heat. Gradually bring the mixture to a boil, whisking continuously.

Once the pudding becomes thick and bubbly, continue to cook it for 1 minute, whisking almost nonstop. Then remove it from the heat and whisk in the vanilla extract. Pour the pudding into a dessert bowl or 6 individual custard cups. Cover with plastic wrap, pressing the plastic directly against the pudding (this will prevent a skin from forming as the pudding cools). Allow the pudding to come to room temperature, then chill it for at least 3 hours before serving. Makes 6 servings.

KIDS' STEPS: Kids can measure ingredients, pour the milk, and add the eggs into the mixing bowl.

Prep time: 10 minutes   Cooking time: 20 minutes   Chilling time: 3 hours

Birthday Sundaes

For your child's birthday dinner, set up a sundae bar, complete with brownies, ice cream, hot fudge sauce, whipped cream, nuts, candy toppings, and cherries. On a table low enough for all family members to see and reach, arrange sundae glasses or bowls, brownies, tubs of ice cream, and toppings (sprinkles, hot fudge sauce, mini candies, maraschino cherries). Invite everyone to build sundaes (a parent can scoop the ice cream). Don't forget a candle for the birthday child!

Chewy Brownies

A PLATE OF THESE moist, rich chocolate bars won't last long. Eat them after dinner tonight, then pack them in lunch boxes for a treat tomorrow.

INGREDIENTS:

- 3 ounces unsweetened chocolate squares
- ½ cup butter (1 stick)
- 3 eggs
- 1 cup sugar
- ¾ cup light brown sugar
- 1½ teaspoons vanilla extract
- ¾ cup all-purpose flour
- ½ teaspoon baking powder
- ¼ teaspoon salt

BROWNIE EXTRAS

- Chocolate, mint, or peanut butter chips
- Chopped pecans or walnuts
- M&M's
- Raisins

DIRECTIONS:

Place the chocolate and the butter in a medium-size saucepan and heat over medium-low, stirring occasionally, until melted and smooth. Set aside until cool (cooling takes 15 minutes or so).

Meanwhile, heat the oven to 350°. Lightly grease a 13- by 9- by 2-inch rectangular baking pan or a 9- by 9-inch square baking pan (the square pan will produce thicker, more cakelike brownies).

In a large bowl, whisk the eggs until foamy. Pour in the sugar and brown sugar and whisk until the mixture is well combined. Whisk in the vanilla extract, then carefully add the cooled chocolate mixture and stir until thoroughly combined.

In a medium-size bowl, stir together the flour, baking powder, and salt. Add this mixture to the egg-and-sugar mixture and beat for about 50 strokes (have the kids count out loud), or until the flour has been fully incorporated and the batter is smooth. Add 1 cup of the brownie extras at this point, if you like.

Pour the batter into the prepared baking pan and bake for 25 to 30 minutes for the 13- by 9- by 2-inch pan, 40 minutes for the 9- by 9-inch pan. Test the brownies for doneness (see the tip below). Cool thoroughly in the pan. Makes 24.

KIDS' STEPS: Kids can unwrap the chocolate and butter, crack the eggs, and grease the pan.

TIP: Brownies are done when a knife inserted into the center of the pan comes out clean.

Prep time: 10 minutes Baking time: up to 40 minutes

Brownie Pizza

TOPPED WITH RED frosting "sauce" and grated white chocolate "cheese," this looks like a real pizza but tastes like a decadent dessert.

INGREDIENTS:

Chewy Brownies batter (see page 88) or a 19.9-ounce box of store-bought brownie mix
2½ cups confectioners' sugar
½ cup butter (1 stick), softened
2½ tablespoons milk
1 teaspoon vanilla extract
Red food-coloring paste (available at kitchen- and party-supply stores)
6 ounces white chocolate
Assorted candies

DIRECTIONS:

Prepare the brownies, but instead of pouring the mixture into a rectangular or square pan, pour it into a lightly greased 12-inch pizza pan. Bake in an oven preheated to 350° for 20 to 30 minutes, or until a knife inserted in the middle comes out clean. Let cool.

Meanwhile, mix up the red frosting "sauce." In a large bowl, cream the confectioners' sugar and butter. Add the milk and vanilla extract and beat until smooth. Add ½ to 1 teaspoon of red food-coloring paste and mix until you have the desired shade (think tomato sauce). Use a spatula or knife to spread the sauce evenly over the cooled "pizza."

Now, you're ready to add the toppings. For white chocolate "cheese," roughly chop or grate (adults only) white chocolate. Sprinkle it over the frosting (your kids may want to add "extra cheese"). For other toppings, add M&M's, chocolate chips, butterscotch chips, or any other favorite candies. Use a pizza cutter to slice the brownie into 16 pieces. Present it in a pizza box (ask a local pizza parlor to give or sell you one). Serve the Brownie Pizza at an after-school gathering, a pizza party, or — most fitting — a Brownie troop meeting. Serves 16.

MY GREAT IDEA
A Kid's Cookbook

"My husband and I love to cook, so naturally we've encouraged our son, Scott, to help in the kitchen since he was a toddler. Now that he's five, he definitely has preferences for certain recipes. So, I've started writing them down in a loose-leaf notebook, with anecdotes about when we made them, who we shared them with, or what Scott said. (For instance, with his favorite brownie recipe, I included his quote, 'I like crummy snacks better, Mom,' meaning, of course, those snacks, like brownies, that make crumbs.) When Scott grows up, he'll have a one-of-a-kind cookbook filled with recipes and memories."

— *Chandra Peters*
Honolulu, Hawaii

KIDS' STEPS: Kids can sprinkle the chopped or grated white chocolate over the frosting and add their favorite candies.

Prep time: 10 minutes Baking time: 30 minutes

Quick Cherry Cheesecake

THIS EASY, no-bake treat combines the flavors of chocolate, cherries, and cheesecake, so it's bound to be a family favorite. Make it with your child as an after-school cooking project and he or she will be proud to serve it for dessert at dinnertime.

INGREDIENTS:

- 1¼ cups chocolate graham cracker crumbs
- ½ cup sugar, divided
- ⅓ cup butter or margarine, melted
- 12 ounces cream cheese, softened
- 2 teaspoons grated lemon peel
- 2 teaspoons vanilla extract
- 2 cups whipped topping (we used Cool Whip)
- 1 20-ounce can cherry pie filling

DIRECTIONS:

In a medium mixing bowl, combine the graham cracker crumbs, ¼ cup of the sugar, and the butter or margarine, mixing well. Firmly press the crumb mixture into the bottom of a 9- by 9- by 2-inch baking pan. Place the pan in the refrigerator to chill while you make the cheesecake filling.

In a large bowl, combine the cream cheese, lemon peel, vanilla extract, and the remaining ¼ cup of sugar. Beat with an electric mixer until light and fluffy, about 2 minutes. Fold in the whipped topping, then spread the mixture onto the chilled crust. Spread the cherry pie filling over the cheese mixture. Chill the cheesecake in the refrigerator until ready to serve. Makes 9 servings.

KIDS' STEPS: Kids can crush the graham crackers, spread the whipped topping onto the crust, and add the cherry pie filling.

Prep time: 15 minutes

Apple Crisp à la Mode

THIS CLASSIC APPLE dessert, with its crunchy topping, is easier to make than pie and just as tasty. Use local apples, such as Rome Beauties or, for a crisper taste, Granny Smiths.

INGREDIENTS:

- 6 apples (or 6 cups of apple slices)
- 1½ cups rolled oats
- ¾ cup brown sugar
- ¼ cup all-purpose flour
- 1 teaspoon cinnamon
- ¼ teaspoon nutmeg
- ¼ teaspoon salt
- ½ cup butter (1 stick), softened
- Whipped cream or ice cream

DIRECTIONS:

Heat the oven to 375° and lightly grease an 8- or 9-inch-square baking pan. Peel, core, and slice the apples and arrange them evenly in the prepared pan.

Place the oats, brown sugar, flour, spices, and salt in a sealable plastic bag, close, and shake until combined. Cut the softened butter into 1-inch pieces and add to the oat mixture. Close the bag again and knead or squeeze until the mixture holds together.

Open the bag and crumble the topping evenly over the apples. Bake the apple crisp for 40 to 45 minutes, or until the topping is golden brown and the juices begin to bubble around the edges. Cool slightly, then serve with whipped cream or ice cream. Serves 6.

KIDS' STEPS: Older kids can peel the apples, while younger kids help cut chunks of apple with a butter knife. Kids can shake, squeeze, and mush the topping in a sealable bag, then crumble the topping over the apples.

QUICK HIT
Instant Baked Apples

Easy enough for older kids to make themselves, this classic dessert (shown above, ready to pop in the microwave) delivers that home-baked apple taste without the oven.

- 1 apple
- 2 teaspoons butter
- 2 teaspoons brown sugar
- 2 teaspoons raisins or chopped walnuts
- 1/8 teaspoon cinnamon

For each serving, use a melon baller to core an apple of any variety (leaving the bottom fourth intact), then place the apple upright in a microwave-safe bowl. Fill the hollowed-out core with a mixture of the butter, brown sugar, walnuts or raisins, and cinnamon. Cover the apple with plastic wrap and microwave it on high for 3 minutes, or until the apple is tender. Use oven mitts to remove it from the microwave. Let the apple cool before you eat it. Serves 1.

Lemon Cups

COOL OFF on a hot summer night with one of these refreshing lemon-ice treats.

INGREDIENTS:

    2 teaspoons lemon zest
    4 to 5 lemons
    ¾ cup fresh lemon juice (from the
       lemons)
    3½ cups water
    1¼ cups sugar
       Mint leaves and lemon zest

DIRECTIONS:

Scrape the 2 teaspoons of zest from one of the lemons, then cut all the lemons in half and juice them. Measure ¾ cup of the juice, reserving the rest for another use. Use a melon baller to remove any remaining pulp from the lemons. Slightly trim the bottom of each lemon so it sits flat, then set them on a plate, cover, and place them in the refrigerator.

In a medium saucepan, combine the water and sugar over medium heat, stirring until the sugar has dissolved. Bring the water to a boil, then add the lemon juice and zest and boil for 2 minutes.

Transfer the liquid to a mixing bowl and allow it to cool to room temperature. Place the bowl in the freezer until the mixture begins to harden, several hours or overnight. Use a fork to break up the ice, then stir it until slushy. Spoon ½ cup of the slush into each lemon half, then cover the halves and freeze until you're ready to serve. Garnish with a mint leaf and lemon zest before serving. Makes 8 to 10 servings.

KIDS' STEPS: Kids can zest and juice the lemon and spoon the slush into the lemon cups.

Prep time: 20 minutes Cooking time: 5 minutes Freezing time: Overnight

Banana Cream Pie

PILED HIGH with layers of pudding, bananas, and whipped cream, this pie is sure to slip onto your family's list of favorites.

INGREDIENTS:
VANILLA PUDDING FILLING:
- ¾ cup plus 2 tablespoons sugar
- ¼ cup plus 2 tablespoons cornstarch
- ⅛ teaspoon salt
- 3 cups milk or half-and-half
- 3 egg yolks
- 2 tablespoons butter, cut into pieces
- 2 teaspoons vanilla extract

CRUST:
- 9 or 10-inch store-bought or homemade graham cracker piecrust

WHIPPED CREAM AND GARNISH:
- 1¼ cups cold heavy cream
- 2 tablespoons confectioners' sugar, sifted
- 2 large ripe bananas (not too ripe)
- Chocolate for garnish

DIRECTIONS:
To make the filling, combine the sugar, cornstarch, and salt in a nonstick medium-size saucepan and whisk until evenly blended. Then whisk in the milk or half-and-half and the egg yolks.

Heat the mixture over medium heat, stirring continuously until it thickens and bubbles, about 5 minutes. Continue cooking for 1 minute more, whisking all the while to keep it from boiling.

Remove the pan from the heat and whisk in the butter one piece at a time. Add the vanilla extract and whisk several more times. Immediately pour the filling into the piecrust, spreading and smoothing it with a wooden spoon.

Gently press a piece of plastic wrap against the filling to keep a skin from forming. Put the pie on a cooling rack and cool to room temperature. Then chill it for at least 6 hours, or overnight.

Ten minutes before you're ready to assemble the pie, chill a mixing bowl and the beaters you'll use to make the whipped cream. Beat the heavy cream in the cold bowl until soft peaks form. Add the confectioners' sugar and continue to beat the whipped cream with a whisk until it is stiff but still smooth. Avoid overbeating it, or the cream will separate, much as it does when you churn butter.

Remove the plastic covering from the pie and use a rubber spatula to spread a thin layer of whipped cream over the pudding. Using a butter knife, quarter the bananas lengthwise, then cut them crosswise into small chunks, letting them fall over the pie in a single layer.

Mound the remaining whipped cream on top of the sliced bananas. Then garnish with shaved chocolate, if you like, and refrigerate the pie until serving time. Makes 8 to 10 servings.

KIDS' STEPS: Kids can measure the ingredients, add the cooled filling to the graham cracker crust, and cut the bananas into small chunks.

Banana Pops

Frozen bananas, chocolate, and crunchy toppings — what more could a kid ask for?

To make a bunch of these tempting treats, cut 4 firm, ripe bananas in half and insert a Popsicle stick halfway into each one. Set the pops on a waxed paper–lined baking sheet and place them in the freezer for 1 hour.

In a small saucepan over very low heat, stir together 1½ cups of semisweet chocolate chips and 2 tablespoons of canola oil until melted. Place toppings, such as shredded coconut, chopped nuts, and sprinkles, in individual bowls.

One at a time, remove the pops from the freezer and, holding them over the saucepan, spoon the chocolate over them. Roll each chocolate-covered banana in a topping, then return it to the freezer to harden for 1 to 2 hours before serving. Makes 8 pops.

Prep time: 30 minutes   Chilling time: 6 hours

Index

Photographers

Reena Bammi: 80

Paul Berg: Front cover (top center), 3, 14, 22, 46, 49, 50, back cover (right)

John Gruen: 4, 9, 68

Jacqueline Hopkins: 16, 17, 19, 20, 21, 77 (top)

Ed Judice: 11, 27 (top), 31, 63, 75 (top), 83, 90, 93

David Martinez: 41 (bottom), 54, 78

Joanne Schmaltz: Front cover (top left, top right, bottom), 10, 12, 25, 26, 27 (bottom), 30, 33 (top), 36, 37, 39, 40, 43, 44, 52, 53 (top), 55, 56, 57, 59, 62, 64, 65, 71, 72, 73 (top), 77 (bottom), 82, 91 (right), 92

Shaffer/Smith Photography: 27 (right), 8, 28, 29, 33 (bottom), 34, 41 (top), 45, 53 (bottom), 60, 61, 66, 67, 70, 73 (bottom), 74, 75 (bottom), 76, 84-89, 91 (left), back cover (left)

Edwina Stevenson: Back cover (center)

Stylists

Bonnie Anderson/Team, Carol Cole, Holly Donaldson/Team, Shannon Dunn, Helen Jones, Janet Miller, Marie Piraino, Karen Quatsoe, Edwina Stevenson, Lynn Zimmerman

Hot Dog Octopus, page 31

Also from **FamilyFun**

FamilyFun Magazine: a creative guide to all the great things families can do together. For subscription information, call 800-289-4849.

FamilyFun Cookbook: a collection of more than 250 irresistible recipes for you and your kids, from healthy snacks to birthday cakes to dinners everyone in the family will enjoy (Disney Editions, $24.95).

FamilyFun Parties: a complete party planner featuring 100 celebrations for birthdays, holidays, and every day (Disney Editions, $24.95).

FamilyFun Birthday Cakes: a batch of 50 recipes for creative party treats (Disney Editions, $10.95).

FamilyFun Boredom Busters: 365 games, crafts, and activities for every day of the year (Disney Editions, $24.95).

FamilyFun Vacation Guide Series: take the vacation your family will remember with our guidebooks, covering New England, Florida, the Mid-Atlantic, the Great Lakes, the Southwest, and California and Hawaii.

FamilyFun.com: get inspired for tonight's dinner and introduce your child to the joys of cooking with more than 2,000 recipes in Recipe Finder. Visit www.familyfun.com/recipes

Get A Whole Year Of Fun!

Only $10.00 for 10 issues

Experience exciting memory-making activities you and your kids will enjoy together.

Quick and easy craft ideas

Proven boredom-buster activities

Recipes kids will eat up

Magical holiday gift, party and costume ideas

Best new toys

...and hundreds and hundreds more fun ideas!

Family-friendly vacations